Here's what people are saying about *Awakening Corporate Soul:*

"Klein and Izzo are leading the vanguard in defining and articulating the territory between work and spirit."

RICHARD J. LEIDER
FOUNDING PARTNER, THE INVENTURE GROUP
AUTHOR OF *THE POWER OF PURPOSE AND REPACKING YOUR BAGS*

"...this book may speak to the heart as well as the mind."

JENNIFER BRANDLON
REVIEWER, *OREGON BUSINESS*

"*Awakening Corporate Soul* is highly recommended for anyone wanting to bring a greater sense of meaning, spirit, creativity, and fulfillment to their work and to their life."

JAMES A. COX
EDITOR IN CHIEF, *THE MIDWEST BOOK REVIEW*

"*Awakening Corporate Soul* is an important text for any leader or individual who wishes to create a strong business culture where personal values and organizational goals can become aligned. Eric Klein and John Izzo are among the major contributors to the critical mass of proponents who are helping reshape the future of business and our lives."

MARK J. DERENGOWSKI
MERCEDES-BENZ OF NORTH AMERICA

"[Awakening Corporate Soul] is all about reconfiguring corporate life so that work is a place people really want to be, a place that releases their full potential!"

NAPRA REVIEW

"Many paths lead to excellence. When the intent of the journey is to love and serve others, these paths lead to hope, healing and awakened soul. *Awakening Corporate Soul* will fill your imagination with ideas that are rich in practicality and your heart with passion for what is right."

PETER MAKOWSKI
CEO
CITRUS VALLEY HEALTH PARTNERS

"Authors Eric Klein and John Izzo describe how to create a satisfied, motivated and committed work force!"

TRAINING MAGAZINE

"Izzo and [Klein] convey a sense of being thoughtful, spiritual, and caring while simultaneously being practical and relevant."

ANN MAHONEY
EDITOR IN CHIEF
ASSOCIATION MANAGEMENT

"Klein and [Izzo] enlighten us with their thoughts about what today's workforce wants."

RONALD SARGENT
DIVIDENDS MAGAZINE

"*Awakening Corporate Soul* can rekindle an unbridled passion for work..."

"It is impossible to build a good organization without first being a good person. When we learn how to embrace and develop the qualities in *Awakening Corporate Soul* we will have also learned how to create greatness in our companies and families. It is time for a global reawakening and this book is the right stimulus. Study it, underline it and discuss it; I have."

"*Awakening Corporate Soul* is one of the most meaningful books I have read. It is a wonderful blend of Spiritual insights and practical applications. It challenged my view of the corporate world and provided me with a blueprint on how to reinvent it.

"This book is a great reminder for all of us that corporations of any kind, whether they be of body or business, can't function usefully without the core essence, or soul, actively taking part."

"*Awakening Corporate Soul* marries the practical and the soulful. In a time when so many of us spend a good part of our paths to Corporate Soul that give leaders who are serious about renewing their organizations a solid way to begin the journey."

ELIZABETH LESSER
CO-FOUNDER, OMEGA INSTITUTE

"The spiritual dimension can never be amputated from work. And yet many organizations try. *Awakening Corporate Soul* will re-ignite the spirit that can increase everyone's commitment to do the right thing and be the best."

KEN BLANCHARD
CO-AUTHOR OF *THE ONE MINUTE MANAGER*

"*Awakening Corporate Soul* shows you how to bring spirituality to the work place. The authors translate ancient wisdom into understandable language and useful methods that can transform our lives and our work."

BARRY HEERMANN, PH.D.
AUTHOR OF *BUILDING TEAM SPIRIT*

"This book changed my life. I read it three times on one week! A Bible (guidebook) for any person who is trying to motivate people and inspire (others to) change. Finally! Clear and actionable answers to 'How do I motivate employees in today's corporate environment?', 'Why haven't our previous efforts succeeded?', and 'How do I become a great leader?'"

L. MICHELLE KISSMAN
LEADERSHIP DEVELOPMENT, AEROSPACE ENGINEER
HUGHES SPACE AND COMMUNICATIONS

"As corporations are the dominant social institution of our era, the authors of this book haven taken on one of the most pressing, noble, and important tasks of our time—to bring greater energy, inspiration, and meaning to corporate culture. *Awakening Corporate Soul* is filled with beautiful and penetrating insights and effective, workable techniques. It greatly enlarged my perspective and direction—I only wish this kind of book had been available twenty years ago!"

KENNETH M. LEE
PRESIDENT, SOFTWARE SOLUTIONS INTERNATIONAL

"*Awakening Corporate Soul* reminds us of truths about our working life that are too easily forgotten, and it offers fresh insights about rediscovering the heart of our work."

WILLIAM KIRKWOOD
PROFESSOR OF COMMUNICATION
EAST TENNESSEE STATE UNIVERSITY

"Managers in corporations know that ongoing success depends on the strength they find within themselves and even more on the inner strength of those they lead. *Awakening Corporate Soul* is a practical and inspiring guide that helps us create work places where we can rediscover the source of our inner strength. Its value is universal. The book is recommended without reservation."

DAVID TURNER
PRESIDENT, THOMSON UNIVERSITY
THE THOMSON CORPORATION

Awakening
Corporate Soul

Awakening Corporate Soul

Four Paths to Unleash the Power of People at Work

Eric Klein & John B. Izzo, Ph.D.

Published by Fairwinds Press

Awakening Corporate Soul

A Fairwinds Book

Canadian Cataloging-in-Publication Data

Klein, Eric , 1953
    Awakening corporate soul: four paths to unleash
    the power of people at work

ISBN 0-9682149-1-6 (bound) - ISBN 0-9682149-3-2 (pbk.)

    1. Employee motivation. 2. Commitment (Psychology).
3. Leadership. I. Izzo, John B. (John Baptist), 1957- II. Title.

HD58.7.K537 1998   658.3'14   C97-901119-1

Editing and text design by: Lead Dog Communications
Jacket design by: Lynn Fleschutz
Jacket photo by: Michael Salas
Printed and bound by: Bang Printing
Eric Klein photo: Trish O'Reilly
John Izzo photo: Robert Bray

Printed and bound in the United States of America
Published in Canada

This book is printed on acid-free paper

Contents

Preface
The Paths of Two Authors

Writing a book with someone else is an ordeal of love by fire. Getting two people to agree on anything, let alone the words that appear on two hundred pages is rewarding but difficult. The book is our co-creation, the preface is ours alone. (We didn't think you'd want to wait another year to read the book!)

John:

For me this is a book about trains. Trains we take in our lives and careers that take us to destinations we never intended. It is about finding ways to be sure the trip we are taking at work is our trip. It is also about how an organization can tap the deepest energies of people at work and how they can overcome the fact that so much of people's capabilities never make it into the work place.

Whenever I read a book, I wonder how an author came to write about that particular subject at that specific time. Here is my story.

In the summer of my twenty-fourth year I received a master's degree from a Presbyterian theological school in Chicago and headed out into the work world. My first full-time job was pastoring a church in a small Ohio town. I had considered other careers—law, politics, acting—but chose ministry over these. Like most people I can't fully recall why, except to say it seemed like the right idea at the time. And I thought I could make a difference and be happy there. My mother had taught me that one should love their work; you spend too much of your time there not to.During my six years of ministry I met a great many people. The time we spent in church and at retreats were valuable but over time I began to sense a disconnect. It was out in the world, if you will, that people discovered meaning and fulfillment. It was in their work they spent 65 percent of their waking life and for many of them, the work drained their spirit and took far more than it ever gave. At the time, it seemed to me that if I were to make a real difference in people's lives, I would have to go where they were to try and discover ways that work could become sacred.

When I left the ministry, having earned most of a Ph.D. in organizational communication I moved into the field of organizational consulting. The decade that followed engaged me in working with executives and companies aimed mostly at improving teamwork, leadership and customer service. Over those ten years I flew over a million miles, earned a good living, and felt my work had made a difference for the companies who had bought my services.

Awakening Corporate Soul

Then one morning an alarm went off (given how much time I spent in hotels it may have been a wake-up call). About 70 percent of my time was spent away from the family I loved. The work was interesting but at the end of the day something wasn't quite right. At first I couldn't put my finger on it. Months of pondering followed until it hit me.

My first career had been about inspiring people, about helping them try to find the best in themselves and discover a life that had meaning. Although the job itself—ministry—turned out to be the wrong train; the yearnings I had experienced in people there were also present in my new work. Here I was trying to help companies improve service, weather change, move into the twenty-first century and the people I encountered, at all levels, had the same yearnings my parishioners had. They wanted something deeper and more profound.

Those moments of reflection led me to a life-changing insight, organizations needed a soul. What's more I wanted to help them get one. It is not that I wanted them to have religion. What they needed was something more than profits, more than team development, more than culture change. Therewas a need to create an environment that could feed the soul.

In the months that followed, I began to put together the relevance of the spiritual traditions as a way of helping leaders reshape the businesses they led.

One of my early mentors used to say "we teach what we most need to learn." Over the years I am convinced this is always true. It is only those struggling with the very thing they teach who experience the bursts of insight required to do that very thing (which is probably why so many teachers and speakers are criticized for notbeing perfect at their own mantras). I wanted more meaning in my work. I wanted a way to make the 65 percent of my waking life spent at work worth the sacrifice of time with family or the tennis court. I wanted a way to make the hours alone in hotels and planes have an even bigger impact.

As I began to speak of these things, I found that leaders and frontline people in many industries felt similar things. They wanted more. They too were being asked to sacrifice a great deal for work and hoped it would ultimately be worth it. It just so happened their companies wanted more from them at the same time.

This book was born out of my honest belief that all the things we try to do in companies—have great service, innovate, find commitment, attract the best people, be more efficient—are only possible when a company offers more than a paycheck. When there is a spirit in the place, great things happen.

Over the past twenty years I have discovered that life is odd, sometimes in the most wonderful way. When I came to California in 1987 and left the ministry in search of another career, I went to a very competent career counselor. She got me out networking with people in organization development. Someone gave me the name of a consultant at General Dynamics who had made the career shift himself years before. They said "you must talk to this guy," but they didn't say why.

We met and he was very gracious. Working from his tiny cubicle in the midst of a literal defense machine, he talked about his own journey, having been trained as a yogi in the Eastern traditions and moving into this new line of management training and consulting. At the time he shared little of the struggles this would bring; perhaps he didn't know it yet.

We met only occasionally over the next eight years until a mutual friend and business partner of mine brought us back together. His name was Eric Klein, and I will ever be grateful that we came together to write this book. It was the work we both needed to learn and so together we began to teach it. In the process our own personal paths have been transformed. We moved each other forward.

I hope the results of our efforts will help you, your company, and your soul. There is little doubt in my mind that any leader or company that walks the paths we outlined here, however imperfectly, will reignite the commitment of themselves and their workers.

No book is complete without thanks. We all owe so much to so many. Although I will leave some important people out, here goes. To my clients over the years who taught me as much as I taught them. To my mother, who did her best as a single parent to ensure that I wanted to make a difference with my time on earth. To my colleagues and friends for support and love, especially Steve and Cindy, who to this day are my anchors. To Leslie, my wife, partner, and friend, without whom I believe this work would have remained inside of me for many more years. And finally to my four children, who reminded me of the light that we all have when we start the journey that lies dormant, always ready to ignite.

J. B. Izzo

Eric:

When I was eleven years old my friend Victor Smallburg and I decided to put on a carnival. It was the end of the summer and the project consumed all our energies. With two other friends we created the events that we thought would be fun: Games of skill including the ring toss, the balance beam, the dart throw, and the nail hammering board; tests of strength—"Which bucket of wet sand can you lift?"; a haunted house in the tool shed, a "roller coaster" —ride blindfolded in a wagon, and a fortune teller's booth. It took the four of us two weeks to get everything ready. Then we stapled posters to telephone poles announcing our Saturday afternoon carnival.

It was a huge success. Victor's yard was filled with people for five hours. Our other friends helped out by manning booths and pulling the ever-popular "roller coaster" ride. That was my first experience of work that engaged my heart, mind, and soul.

After high school I moved to Boulder, Colorado, into a house where everyone was studying and practicing yoga. I met my future wife at a silent meditation retreat. I dove full-time into the spiritual search and like many young people of the time turned away from the main stream culture. I figured work and the world of work could wait for me to be enlightened. Then I met my spiritual teacher.

In one of our first meetings I asked him what I needed to do to grow spiritually. He told me, "You need to work and bring home the soybean bacon." Difficult as that was to hear, I had to admit he was right. I believed my life work was to help people understand themselves and grow spiritually. I just wasn't sure of how to translate that belief into the marketplace.

I bounced from job to job for a number of years, all the while teaching yoga and meditation at yoga centers, conferences, retreats, and university extension programs. I loved working with adults and helping them make tangible changes that improved their lives. When I discovered the field of management training I felt like a traveler returning home. Here was an established discipline where I could help people make personal breakthroughs and enhance their professional success. Here was a field where my talents, values, and interests could come together at last.

I secured a position with a small training firm in South Bend, Indiana, that was pioneering a new communication discipline called Neuro-Linguistic Programming (NLP). Working at the Midwest Institute of NLP was like being immersed in afull-time personal growth workshop. The training I received has been central to my life and work not only in terms of information but in terms of the spirit of learning that permeated the organization. I met passionate professionals who are still my good friends.

But the weather and culture of a small Midwestern town didn't suit my family. My wife, son, and I moved to California where, after two months of furious networking, I was hired as a management trainer for a division of General Dynamics. Ironically, I was hired because my new boss, Michele Tamayo, had an intense curiosity about meditation. She trusted her instincts on the fact that I could translate my meditation and NLP background into practical training programs for GD managers. She was right. My coworker Gary Winters and I created a management university that helped hundreds of managers develop themselves and their teams.

It was while at GD that I met my co-author John Izzo. He was new to town and networking as I had done a few years earlier.

The call of entrepreneurship and the mismatch between my values and those of the General Dynamics organization led to a parting of the ways after five years of hard work. For almost ten years as an independent consultant I have continued to explore how to incorporate the spiritual dimension into the work I do with leaders. The more experience I gain, the more I am convinced that the solutions to all our organizational problems come from the soul. No amount of superficial tinkering can produce sustainable results. The past two years have brought a big shift in my work. Maybe it has to do with getting older, but I feel more comfortable talking about things spiritual with managers and leaders. I make room for the soul in my conversations, workshops, and meetings. This book is a way of extending the conversation into the world.

Writing a book about the soul at work has been a challenging process. Many times, I have recalled this story from the life of Mahatma Gandhi. Once, a grandmother brought her grandson to Gandhi. The boy it seemed had an insatiable appetite for sugar that was threatening his health. "Please," she asked Gandhi, "tell him to stop eating sugar. He has so much respect for you. He will listen to what you say."

"Please go away and come back in four days," replied Gandhi. The woman and her grandson did as requested. On the fourth day they returned and Gandhi looked into the boy's eyes. "Stop eating sugar. It will harm your body," he said.

After a short silence, the grandmother asked, "Sir, why did you ask us to wait four days before speaking to my grandson?"

"Madame," Gandhi replied, "four days ago I had not myself stopped eating sugar."

To write a book on awakening Corporate Soul could be a tremendous act of hubris, calling down the wrath of the gods. It would be if it were a written in the voice of authority, telling you what you had to do. But it isn't written in that voice because I haven't yet stopped eating sugar. I haven't yet awakened fully. I am simply on the journey of awakening, walking the pathways of the soul. I think we all are.

At the same time, I don't want to tell you to come back in four days. I don't want to wait until I'm more enlightened to engage in this critical conversation about the soul and work. I'm concerned we may not get another chance to talk.

I have decided to let you know about what I've learned so far on the journey from my eleven year old carnival to the board rooms of corporate America. In some ways it is all quite simple. The essence of what makes great work never changes. The soul is still nourished by the bread of wisdom and the wine of love.

You have the answer and energy you seek deep within your soul. I hope this book will remind you of what you already know and will compel you to take the next step on your spiritual path. Your soul will smile when you do.

I have been enriched by working on this book with my co-author John Izzo. He held the mirror of truth up for me to see myself. It wasn't always easy to look, but I am grateful he kept the mirror in hand. John, you have helped me fulfill my dream. I was immeasurably aided by the two greatest and most benefic influences in my life: my spiritual teacher Goswami Kriyananda, who has shown me wisdom in action, and my wife Deborah Bliss, who is my greatest and truest friend. May we continue to walk the path together.

Eric Klein

Awakening
Corporate Soul

"The soul is where the inner and the outer world meet."
—NOVALIS

"Something opens our wings.
Something makes boredom and hurt disappear.
Someone fills the cup in front of us.
We taste only sacredness."
—RUMI

1

The Commitment Crisis
& Corporate Soul

The spiritual dimension can never be amputated from work. It can be ignored but never removed. The words Carl Jung carved over the door of his country retreat, "Called or not called God is present," remind us that even when we are most oblivious the spiritual dimension is closer than our breath. In a sense, these words are invisibly carved over the entrance to every company, over every desk and work station. It is time to pay attention to the most neglected—and the most essential—aspect of our work life.

There is, at this time, both a crisis and a longing that permeates organizations across North America. We call one the commitment crisis, the struggle of organizations and their leaders to discover ways to ignite commitment and performance in a rapidly changing insecure climate. The other is an awakening that is slowly occurring within traditional businesses—the awakening of the Corporate Soul. It is a nascent movement that seeks to reclaim the spiritual impulse that is at the heart of work. It is about people wanting work to have meaning and even more, to engage more of them at the deepest levels of their capacity and desire.

This book reflects our experiences as participants in both the crisis of commitment and the soulful awakening that is opening into a new world of work.

Taking a Trip to Nowhere

When we first heard this true story in an airport lounge we thought it was just a funny anecdote. But truth and wisdom can come in unexpected packages. Over time we saw that what we have come to call the "train story" captures a powerful truth about the challenge leaders and organizations are facing.

The story was told to us by a man who grew up in a small farming town in the Midwest. Trains passed through the town every day on their run to the city some 40 miles north. It was the habit of the older, more daring boys to occasionally hitch a ride on a passing car and spend the day in the city. The storyteller's cousin Jack was one of those intrepid travelers. One day, craving cookies from a certain bakery in the city, he jumped a train. Covering himself in some discarded burlap, he fell asleep. Unfortunately for him, he slept too long. Hours later he awakened in a cold, darkened car. The door was locked—from the outside. And he was in a refrigeration car accompanying several dozen sides of beef, rattling toward an unknown destination. He spent several days in the chilly company of his silent bovine companions only to be rescued by an alert yard man who thought he heard muffled cries of "Help, let me out!" coming from one of the meat cars. Cousin Jack emerged from his ordeal into the light of a bright Oregon afternoon, cold, shaken, and several thousand miles from his intended destination. He wondered if the cookies were worth it.

The story is a metaphor for the crisis and longing gripping businesses today. It is about how to unlock the potential in their people. It is about whether someone who feels "locked up" inside our organization for forty hours each week can perform at the level they must for us to stay competitive.

Many people began their working lives like cousin Jack. They just wanted to go for a short ride into town. They began with little more than a "craving for cookies" in the form of a salary capable of feeding their families. Many of them wake up years later to discover themselves riding in the dark, rattling toward some uncertain destination. It is easy to live someone else's life at work and to feel that our "souls" and much of our potential at work are locked away.

We know there is something engaging about this story because whenever we tell it in a corporate seminar, the heads of leaders and workers nod in agreement. Leaders know they can't compete with a company full of people whose passions are not ignited and who lie half asleep crying to get out. All of us know, that we give too much of our lives to work not to listen to the cries from within.

Leaders and workers today have begun to hear the cries for help that are coming from inside themselves. These cries are the voice of the soul, muffled and shivering, but still alive, wanting to be let out. Called or not the soul is there. Who will take responsibility for letting it out? Consider what level of commitment or innovation is possible in an organization where the soul is virtually locked in a cold storage container.

One needn't go anywhere to find Corporate Soul. It doesn't exist in a secret text or a hidden monastery. Soul is where you are. And for most of the day that means at work. As Jewish theologian Abraham Joshua Heschel has said, "God is hiding in the world and our task is to let the divine emerge from our deeds." Leadership, in this context, begins by acknowledging the presence of the soul. When it comes to awakening the Corporate Soul leadership is based on understanding that the soul wants to shine through us and illuminate our work and workplaces.

Time for a Wake-Up Call

"We are asleep until something wakes us up," according to Bill Marriott of hotel fame. This was as true for us, as for any beginning seeker. We have both been successful management consultants for over a decade. In retrospect it is clear that the race for success became an alternative to deeper searching. We became adept at ignoring the sounds of our own wake-up calls for a number of years. If the soul was calling us between nine and five, we were too busy to answer. It was easy to be distracted by the demands, deadlines, and excitement of building our business. But one evening as we sat in hotel rooms on opposite sides of the country, we each became acutely aware of a deeper longing within our souls that could no longer be ignored. As we talked, we recognized the need to find greater alignment between our highest and most precious values and the work we were involved in with managers on a day-to-day basis. That evening became a turning point in our journey.

Before that, our routine was simple. After spending the day with leaders, managers, and assorted corporate warriors searching for ways to improve quality and squeeze out more profits, we would return to our hotel rooms and pursue our own spirituality. We were doing good work, helping people and organizations, yet there was something missing. We talked about it and for a long time were unable to name the longing. It was a slow process that brought us to the realization that our weariness had a spiritual origin and that the same stirrings were being felt by our clients.

Many of the leaders we worked with wanted something deeper as much as we did. Yet in the meeting rooms where we spent our days, no one put the longing into words. Was it because it was too vague or because it was really all too clear what bringing this inner longing to consciousness would mean? As Richard, the vice president of a regional bank told us, "I knew the work was suffocating my soul but to admit it would be too devastating; it would mean that I had to do something about it!"

The Commitment Crisis

The month after that soul-turning evening, we attended a conference featuring many of the fastest-growing technology companies in North America. The conference closed with a panel of chief executive officers who were asked, "What will be the greatest challenge facing your organization five years from now?" More than half of the ten CEOs said something like, "We will be struggling with how to reignite commitment and help people find meaning in their work." The commitment crisis is an insidious and powerful disease that is affecting those who work in corporations.

From the corporate perspective the struggle is for basic survival fueled by a never-ending search for lower costs, increased productivity, innovation, and superlative performance. Companies that can no longer offer security or pay raises grapple with how to foster loyalty and commitment. With security gone as a carrot, with a new generation of workers looking for more from work than money, with personal balance becoming a major issue for both men and women, and with growing burnout at all levels, the modern organization is struggling with how to attract and keep top people let alone motivate them.

But from the human perspective the crisis is highly personal and threatens the inner sense of purpose, caring, and vitality that makes work meaningful. Millions of workers feel burned out, overworked, and stressed to the max with a deep sense of having sacrificed too much of their personal lives for the corporate good. A quest for something more is brewing inside workers from the shop floor to the top of the corporate ladder. It is a crisis of soul that can only be resolved by the awakening of what we call Corporate Soul.

It is important to see the way this crisis cuts in two directions. It is highly personal even while its effects are evident in "the numbers." At a recent seminar, one woman said, "Every once and a while in the desert of my work I find an oasis that helps me see why I am putting in so much time and effort. The hard part is that there seem to be more and more miles between each oasis."

Marcia, a health care vice president told us, "The light at the end of the tunnel has fizzled out." Mark, who heads a large printing company confessed, "We have put people through so much—downsizing, right sizing, and reengineering—that job security is a term reserved for stand-up comics. I'm not sure how you develop commitment anymore. Even for myself."

We believe that reclaiming and awakening the Corporate Soul is the foundation of sustainable competitiveness because the soul is the very source that allows people to endure and create in uncertain times. As David Whyte aptly puts it in his work, *The Heart Aroused,* when describing most organizational responses to crisis, "for all their emphasis on the bottom line, they are adrift from the very engine at the center of a person's creativity...they cultivate a workforce unable to respond with personal artistry to the confusion of market change." The temptation to dismiss the soul as too soft to deal with real world pressures is short sighted. Ironically, the tougher the times the more soul must be present to meet the challenges. As the sage Lao Tsu has written, "The soft overcomes the hard; the gentle overcomes the rigid. Everyone knows this is true, but few can put it into practice."

What Is Corporate Soul?

If the phrase Corporate Soul conjures up images of workers praying in the corridors or of Gregorian chants filling the lunch room (or worse, motivational slogans while you are on hold when calling your local department store), think again. Corporate Soul is not a theological concept. It is a term we use to describe the experience of coming fully alive at work. Corporate Soul is foremost an experience of touching a deeper level of vitality, inspiration, meaning, and creativity—more than just "doing my job" implies.

Awakening Corporate Soul is about bringing the deepest and most dynamic energies into work, not institutionalizing a particular belief system. Soul, as we use the term, signifies the basic vital life energy that underlies and animates all human activity. The inspiration of an artist, the passion of an entrepreneur, the commitment of a parent, and the curiosity of a scientist—all these qualities and more arise from the matrix of the soul. Corporate Soul is the expression of this primary life-giving energy in work and the workplace. When Corporate Soul is awake, work flourishes, overflows, and manifests as productivity, creativity, innovation, and inspiration.

We use the words Corporate Soul attentive to the many reactions this term can trigger. The word soul has been burdened with an overabundance of connotations. It has been used in so many ways by so many groups that for many modern people "soul" has become an appealing but ambiguous mystery. We do not want to become mired in theological wordsmithing and cannot follow the philosopher Ludwig Wittgenstien's counsel,

"Concerning that which cannot be talked about, we should not say anything." Rather we want to define terms in a way that supports our intention of renewing and transforming work life and work places.

Can a Corporation Have a Soul?

The awakening of Corporate Soul begins with the individual. They open to the wealth of resources that is the soul. But when an awakening person arrives Monday morning at an environment that is inimical to soul, they withdraw. The blossoming matrix closes up. The resources go untapped. That is why individual soul awakening is not enough. In Judaism the term *Tikkun Olan,* or healing of the world, makes it clear that no one can be healed alone. Isolated fulfillment is a contradiction in terms. We are healed through and for one another. The native American author Jamake Highwater uses the word *orenda* to refer to the tribal soul or the tribal fire. There are times that the *orenda* burns brightly—when the people are united in a common purpose, a shared ritual, or a communal celebration. And there are times when the *orenda* is dim—in times of unresolved discord, confusion regarding direction, and fear.

In the same way, the state of the Corporate Soul of one organization is not the same as that of another. For some organizations, it is clear the Corporate Soul is drowsy; in others it appears passed out. The degree of Corporate Soul "wakefulness" will be reflected in the quality of commitment and excitement (or lack of it) that is present in the workforce, and ultimately in the competitiveness of the business. Albert Camus wrote,

"Without work all life goes rotten—but when work is soulless, life stifles and dies." When an organization's soul sleeps, the people in that organization lose the sense of their purpose and place in the market. They become fundamentally impaired, going through the motions of their work without the breath of life.

We understand Corporate Soul best by simply walking into any office. Immediately there is a palpable sense of the soul of that place, the inner nature of the enterprise. One is aware of certain defining qualities reflected in the physical space, the organizational structure, the language, and behaviors of the people you meet. But behind these outer expressions there is a basic energy—the Corporate Soul of that workplace. If we are honest we can feel the "soul" in a place from the moment we enter it. Though a final definition of soul may be impossible to reach, recognizing the power of its presence for ourselves and our organizations is essential. As Albert Schweitzer wrote, "I have never seen a good definition of soul, but I know it when I feel it." So too we know when we have it in our own work.

Reclaim the Soul

Many organizations today have been shocked by the diagnosis of "change or die." Workers have been thrown into an unfamiliar world where security is an illusion and leaders struggle with how to inspire commitment amidst so much chaos. As the familiar economic and social forms disintegrate, there is, more than ever, a need for grounding organizational life in the enduring values that are the soul's natural province. Perhaps organizations can learn from the experiences seriously ill people report of the incredible stability and direction that awareness of their own deeper purpose provides as they struggle with the shock of life-threatening illness. Through recognizing and reclaiming the deeper meaning of their lives, these patients are able to embrace reality, take action, and live in ways that are more authentic and enriching.

Certainly organizations do not have to wait for a life-threatening condition to begin reorienting toward a more soulful direction. Just seeing the inevitability of change and gratefully choosing to live vitally in the face of impermanence is a powerful leadership stance available at any moment. More than ever, in the marketplace, it is clear that there are no promises. Change is the status quo. For leaders the challenge is to see such instability as the ideal conditions for engaging the soul of the organization. By anchoring their business solutions in that deeper source, by reclaiming the spiritual impulse at the heart of work, the human commitment and energy required to carry out a truly sustainable strategy in the midst of relentless change is released.

Naming the Yearning

Such a yearning is emerging in the workplace today. Behind the anger and cynicism there is a longing to integrate soul life and work life, to create a unified fabric that weaves together the inner and outer worlds. On the surface we accept a "Dilbert" view of the world of work replete with tremendous wit and soul-numbing cynicism that nothing better is possible. At a more profound level, the level of our soul, we all know that it must be possible to find our best at work.

Meister Eckhart, a great mystic who understood the daily experience of his parishioners, said, "To be right a person must do one of two things. Either he must learn to have God in his work and hold fast to Him there, or he must give up his work altogether. Since, however, we cannot live without work, we must learn to keep God in everything we do whatever job or place." We would add that just as one cannot live without work, one cannot truly work without soul.

There may be a certain amount of fear associated with the expression of our soul yearnings. After all, these are tight times and the company may not want someone around who has soft and fuzzy ideas about soul. With stress high and fuses short, people may have little patience for this stuff. One may have this fear as the CEO facing the board and shareholders or a front-line worker facing a hard-driving middle manager.

For us the fear was about credibility. Would anyone take us seriously once we introduced the notion of Corporate Soul as fundamental to organizational renewal? Before our working with organizations, we had both begun our careers in highly spiritual endeavors, John as a Presbyterian minister and Eric as a yoga and meditation teacher. Years later while the spiritual dimension of our lives were still active personally, the focus of our professional activities had shifted to the corporate arena. Our discovery of Corporate Soul brought two parallel aspects of our lives together into a balanced whole.

In practical terms this meant opening ourselves up to asking questions and pursuing actions that were not in the mainstream of organizational change. Overcoming our own hesitancy to bring up deeper questions in the workplace required vulnerability and courage. It meant we would have to strip away the shield of our so-called professional image and speak from a place that was unprotected. t. s. eliot, recalling the teachings of Saint John of the Cross, wrote, "If you wish to arrive at a place you do not know, you must take the path you do not know." Such was our dilemma and the dilemma of many of our clients.

As we began our journey in earnest we wondered, How do leaders break through to discover the soul of their own work? How does an organization begin to nourish and feed its own deepest possibilities? How does the workplace move from cynicism to a fresh vitality that skillfully rides the waves of change?

Not Another Management Fad, Please

What became clear was that traditional organizational change efforts do not address the deeper soul levels. There are great techniques and procedures for measuring, assessing, and changing organizational behavior, structure, and policies. And although we had seen positive changes occur using these methods, they did not touch the soul directly.

When we first started discussing Corporate Soul with people in organizations we got one of two basic reactions. Some people dismissed it as new age nonsense. This did not disturb us much. But what did get us thinking were those who said that corporate soul was just a new word for empowerment, quality improvement, team-building, visioning, and so on. This was critical for us to understand.

Is this just a new term for familiar change techniques? The best answer is that what we are talking about is a deeper level of change. Teams, empowerment, family-friendly policies, and such are all valid ways to create organizations capable of both engaging commitment and maintaining competitive advantage. Yet such techniques can only take an organization so far. There can be teams but not community; clearly defined outcomes but no real sense that the work contributes to anything significant. One can institute flexible work hours but still have a workplace where people cannot be themselves or speak the truth without fear. Awakening Corporate Soul deals with a level of change that is more profound and that touches the deepest aspects of our being.

We can illustrate the nature of this shift in terms of a marital relationship. A couple may learn communication skills that change the way they argue, make decisions, and requests of each other. They may in addition establish a special "date night" and reorganize their schedules to have more time together. But communication skills and schedule changes, as important as they are, do not make a lasting or fulfilling marriage. There is another level of awareness and development that must be in place for a marriage to sustain and flourish. This level goes beyond techniques and includes mutual respect, self-responsibility, shared values, and the willingness to be fully seen. Profound communication arises naturally when these deeper changes are in place.

So too are empowerment, teams, and organization development helpful tools for companies and leaders. They have produced some positive and worthwhile changes in both corporate competitiveness and integrity. Still, even the best companies wind up filled with workers who are skeptical about the possibilities for change. Hence, awakening Corporate Soul is about going deeper to reconfigure corporate life in ways that can bring out the deepest human potential. The bulk of this book is about walking the paths that lead to such a workplace.

Work Is Sacred

A sound starting place for the discovery of soul at work is the recognition that work is sacred for most people, however hidden this fact may be from most workers and leaders. In the Zen Buddhist tradition a period of time is set aside each day for physical work such as gardening, carpentry, and other tasks required to maintain a monastery in good working order. It is written that the Master Hyakujo joined his students each day during this period of work. As the Master aged his students felt it was inappropriate for him to subject himself to such labors. They spoke with him but their suggestion was brushed aside. One monk took the matter into his own hands and hid the Master's tools. The Master spent the next day in his room, sitting quietly. When the attendant brought him his meals, Hyakujo nodded politely but took no food. He simply sat. After three days of delivering uneaten food, the attendant pleaded, "Master, why do you not eat?"

Hyakujo replied, "A day of no work is a day of no food."

As this story suggests work itself is spiritual food. To work is to eat that food. The soul requires a sense of being in the world, of having a place and making a contribution. To a great degree this comes through work. It is not possible to speak of soul at work or soulful workplaces until we recognize that for most people work is about spirit as much as salary. To see work as just a way to earn a paycheck is to starve the soul. Leaders who see those who work for them as primarily on a quest for a salary miss out on the actions that can ignite sustainable commitment.

A 1996 *Fortune* magazine survey indicated that eight out of ten people would continue working even if they became rich enough that they did not need the money. Why? The three most frequent responses were: to have a sense of service, to help themselves and others grow, and to perfect their skills. Of course, many said they would modify the nature of their work to conform more with their spiritual, social, or artistic values. When freed from the monetary requirements, most choose to continue feeding their soul via working.

At one of our seminars, Lisa stood up and shared, "You know, no one ever said on their death bed, 'I wish I'd spent more time at the office.'" Although we granted her the odds, having not been at enough bedsides to know, we probed more deeply by suggesting her joke spoke more to the fact that work, as currently designed, does not nourish the soul than to the fact that work in and of itself is not central to spiritual life.

An ancient hymn from the *Rig Veda,* the oldest scripture of India, says, "Let not the thread of my song be cut while I still sing. Let not my work end before its completion." There is a fire within the soul that wants to burn to the end. We want to invest our time in work that calls forth the greatness we sense within the soul. Certainly Hyakujo's story points to the inseparable nature of work and spiritual life. In fact, all the wisdom traditions point out that work is integral to fulfilled living. By separating work from the soul we are, in a real sense, avoiding one of our most basic drives.

Strategies for the Soul

The awakening of the soul is neither a matter of chance nor one that is completely under the control of the will. In all spiritual traditions this paradox is well known. In traditional paths there are practices and techniques that are used to rouse the sleeping soul and to infuse it with the vitality of its true inheritance. Whether prayer, meditation, or other well-defined forms of spiritual work, the traditions are clear that the pursuit of an awakened soul is not a random, ill-defined process. One meditation master has said, "Enlightenment is an accident, but some activities make you accident prone." The Corporate Soul may not be awakened by sending out a memo, but there are definite activities that promote and accelerate awakening.

Over our years of consulting we have spent months of our lives helping leaders craft strategies of various kinds: market strategies, technology strategies, human resource strategies, cost-cutting strategies, and customer service strategies. But how many take time to develop and practice soul strategy? Just as in our personal lives, when the demands of a relentless schedule drive out time for soul work, so too, in organizations is the soul left to fend for itself. What organization would let market share fend for itself? Surely such a passive strategy would be transparently absurd. The same can be said for the soul.

When the soul is trapped in the dark box car, expecting it to fend for itself is foolish. The soul is awakening in organizations. It is a wake-up call. The realization that riding after cookies is not enough has dawned for many. Listening to the call is the first step. Then taking action and crafting strategies of awakening must follow.

Exercise: Taking the Pulse of the Soul of Your Workplace

How awake is the Corporate Soul in your workplace? What are the signs that reveal this condition in your organization?

_____

_____

_____

_____

_____

_____

_____

_____

_____

_____

_____

Exercise: What Is Corporate Soul?

We must begin by naming the yearning. How would you define having soul in your work? Write a sentence or two focusing on the key words that describe the feeling you desire at work.

_____

_____

_____

_____

_____

_____

Now, as a leader, try to describe what it would mean for your organization to be one that has Corporate Soul. Again, focus on key words that describe the feeling you would desire to be true of your workplace.

_____

_____

_____

_____

_____

_____

"All mystics speak the same language because
they come from the same country."
—Louis Claude de Saint-Martin

"Travelers, there is no path,
Paths are made by walking."
—Antonio Machado

Monks, Monasteries, & Modern Business

This book did not begin as a business book based on spiritual traditions. Although we have both been students of these traditions our entire lives and felt that they offered practical guidance for the corporate life, we resisted using them as a foundation. It was not until we began talking to our clients, many of whom were not students of the traditions per se, that we began to see the clear connection between the struggle of the modern corporation for commitment and the wisdom found in the spiritual traditions. The very things people told us engaged them at work and unlocked their deepest capabilities—a sense of service, being in the moment, true community, personal alignment and artistry—were also the focus of many of the East and West traditions we had spent a decade pondering and practicing.

Still, we put the traditions at the center of our work with some trepidation. The "S" words—soul, spirit, sacred—are not common vernacular in the business lexicon. Would readers and clients oppose them in the fear that religion and work were being mixed? Would these principles be passed off as New Age fuzziness that had no relevance to the tough-minded corporate market? Would we be able to communicate the tremendous value the wisdom traditions bring to healing the underlying ailment affecting organizational life?

Go to the Source

The wisdom traditions contain the repository of human learning regarding the soul. The traditions are the record of our collective striving toward and realization of the sacred. Great spiritual geniuses from every culture have had their teachings preserved in sacred texts. In the face of such resources, we do not need to wait for the next management buzz word. The deeper guidance we seek is already available.

In his classic work on the world's spiritual traditions, *The Perennial Philosophy,* Aldous Huxley pointed out that beneath the differing forms and rituals of the diverse traditions is a hidden spring flowing with a common wisdom. When we strip off the cultural layer, spiritual teachings reveal a consistent core of wisdom. This core is the source of enduring guidance.

It is not our aim to turn businesses into monasteries or to suggest religion belongs in the workplace. Religion is neither within the realm of corporate concern nor the concern of this book. Rather, we are interested

Awakening Corporate Soul

in the spiritual traditions and their powerful core of wisdom. Calling upon the traditions is reclaiming the wisdom of the ages that teaches how we can be our best. Such a resource cannot be ignored if we wish to truly improve our organizations. With reverence we introduce the traditions as a much-needed resource.

There is a tendency for business leaders to be seduced by each new fad and management fashion. Consequently, it may seem old-fashioned but radical to suggest that the answers to the most fundamental questions of motivation, community, and commitment are readily available in the timeless wisdom of all traditions. But the traditions have survived precisely because people—and human dilemmas—have changed so little. Certainly the form of the challenges have changed, especially with advances in technology, globalization, and market shifts.

Why not seek guidance in teachings that have informed countless seekers for thousands of years? Why bypass this treasure house of insight developed over centuries? The lasting ability of the wisdom traditions to inform and guide human experience testifies to their inherent usefulness. William O'Brien, former CEO of Hanover Insurance writes, "Many managers do not achieve the excellence they are capable of simply because they have not devoted enough time to reflecting on the application of the wisdom of the ages to their professional responsibilities."

Buddha & Burnout

Early in his consulting practice Eric discovered how the spiritual traditions could reignite commitment at work.

He was part of a team of trainers delivering a five-day leadership program to members of a Fortune 500 organization. After the first session it became clear they were dealing with some unhappy people, most of whom were in middle management positions and felt caught, victimized, overburdened, and threatened by the pressures of their jobs. Consequently, it was with some trepidation that Eric headed off to his second assignment as the solo trainer for twenty managers of a division located in the Northeast. It was February and the icy landscape outside matched Eric's expectations for the session. Entering the training room on the first day, Eric looked into forty unresponsive eyes and felt a wave of anger pass through him. "I'm not going to let them get me down. I'll show them!" he thought. He pulled out his most motivational stories, his most humorous anecdotes, his most probing techniques. It was useless. A cloud of cynicism and resignation still hung in the air.

Driving back to his hotel room Eric observed the decaying mill town, the peeling paint, the abandoned cars. In his hotel room, as though in diabolical conspiracy with his sinking mood, the shower refused to give hot water. Later that evening while reading a book on Buddhism, Eric came across a description that so closely matched his own mood he was taken aback. The passage catalogued the traits that make up the suffering mind: anger, bitterness, self-righteousness, and the foolishness of seeing others and the external world in general as the source of one's problems. Adopting such a view, the text pointed out, is a recipe for extreme frustration. Experiencing life in this state of mind was called "all appearances arising as the enemy." Eric realized he had been busily populating his world with enemies—the trainees and all their managers, the hotel staff, the plumbing, the people who got him into this job in the first place!

The text went on to describe the way out of this self-made hell, which is to see experience as a teacher and to listen deeply and thus transform even the most challenging situation into an occasion for learning. When he entered the classroom the next day his defensive posture had been replaced by one of openness and curiosity. What had appeared as resistance the previous day looked more like realistic frustration with a program that had been imposed from "above." Leaving his planned agenda, Eric asked, "What would make the remaining four days together meaningful and useful for you?" Because the feeling behind the question was genuine (rather than just a technique) the group responded. The wall between Eric and the managers in the program began to dissolve. Together the managers explored the nature of their frustrations and challenges. They began to identify their own needs for growth and learning. Several managers commented on the power of the mind to shape experience. "There are plenty of things here that need to change," admitted one participant, "but for me the first one is my own attitude."

The words of an ancient wisdom text had transformed a dreary training session dominated by cynicism into an opportunity for true breakthroughs.

Language & Business Renewal

When we first began a serious inquiry into the development of Corporate Soul we took notice of the language used in the corporate world. The everyday language of business has fenced out the soul, the spiritual, and the sacred. The mere mention of these "s" words in the meeting rooms of most organizations is in violation of an unwritten taboo. After all, the thinking goes, this is business! What place does the soul have here? Amazingly, it has come to be unacceptable to incorporate our most profound impulses and thoughts into the very environment where we spend half our waking hours and the majority of our energy. The lexicon of business focuses on easily measured deliverables. At the same time, straightforward truth-telling is supplanted by euphemisms such as right sizing and career-assessment opportunities.

Language is powerful. It does not merely describe but also shapes reality. Language becomes the filter through which we perceive the world. If our language excludes the soul we will be unable to envision the real possibility of a soulful workplace. As a consequence of diminished language, the realities of the soul are not welcomed in most companies. Yet one of the axioms of the wisdom traditions is that whether we live in the mountains of Tibet, on the banks of the Jordan, or in a major metropolitan area, we will always need to face and resolve certain essential human questions. Environment may differ, but the fundamental human agenda remains unchanged.

In our work with managers the issues that arise again and again are those ancient questions of the human soul: What am I here for? How can I balance my life? What is the purpose of this work? How does it fit into the larger picture of my life? What does it mean to lead? To follow? To serve? What are the roles of courage, detachment, and compassion at work? Although such questions are at the root of many organizational crises, there is often no forum in which to examine these issues. Further, there is often no "acceptable" language for voicing these concerns.

One reason to use the wisdom traditions as a foundation for reigniting commitment at work is because they provide us with a language for the soul. The soul requires a language deeper than "quarterly profits, annual reviews, competitive analysis," and so on. As we move ourselves and our organizations into the global marketplace that demands creativity, commitment, community, and an unrelenting adaptation to new circumstances, we will need a way of calling forth the greatest of human intentions in ourselves and others. This requires the kind of language the wisdom traditions offer. Studies on creativity and innovation have shown that the very act of using a new language breaks old patterns and lifts us into new vistas.

Resistance to more soulful language can reach comical proportions. Recently, Mary, one of our colleagues, was seated next to a senior executive of a Fortune 100 firm. During their in-flight conversation about change and the need to foster greater adaptability among workers, Mary asked what she thought was a simple question: "What are you doing in your company to help people identify how their personal values align with the company's aims?"

The executive looked stunned. "It's illegal," he told her, "to ask people to look at their personal values during work."

A new language is required if businesses are to tap a deeper level of engagement. Words such as community, meaning, service, contribution, joy, passion, vocation, and soul must gain equal footing with more familiar words like teamwork, outcomes, value-added, job, and performance. Imagine what might happen in any business simply by the infusion of a new glossary, one that appeals to people's deepest aspirations, creativity, and convictions.

Walking the Talk

Our spiritual and work lives had been running along parallel tracks for years. We come from divergent spiritual traditions. John followed a Western path and was a Presbyterian minister. Eric looked to the East for his inspiration and spiritual practice. After years of training with his guru Eric became a teacher of yoga and meditation. We had pursued our spiritual paths for over two decades while developing active careers as organizational consultants. And although the values and insights of our spiritual lives came through our consulting work, there was still a disconnection. A thin but definite wall separated the spiritual self from the professional self. Whereas we once argued this was only appropriate and led to better results for our clients, the more we listened to the voice of Corporate Soul the less true this seemed.

In meeting after meeting when the going got tough, when our clients would become cynical or frustrated, we would wonder privately, "Are we addressing the real issues here? Isn't there something more fundamental that needs to be discussed and resolved?" It was not until we actively began to explore how the wisdom traditions could be related to the struggles of modern corporate warriors that breakthroughs began.

For John, one of those moments of insight came in the midst of a multi-year contract focused on improving customer service. In a three-day offsite meeting with the organization's managers, he casually mentioned his first career as minister and leader of spiritual retreats. This was the first time most of them had heard about this aspect of John's background. During breaks over the three days many of the managers came over to John and expressed a desire to hear how John related spirituality to corporate life and success. It seemed many had been waiting for someone to invite the deeper aspects of their being into the office.

The level of interest and excitement in the room shifted to a new level. By mentioning the spiritual traditions people felt empowered to push their conversation, questioning, and commitment to a deeper level. It was one of the most powerful sessions they had ever had.

Stories of Corporate Soul

As it became clear that there was a definite thirst for deeper ways of working we began to search for how to skillfully bring the wisdom traditions into the workplace. It was our clients who helped us discover viable methods for awakening Corporate Soul. At our workshops and during speeches, we asked several thousand people to describe times when they were fully alive at work, when soul permeated their corporate life. We wanted to know what brought soul forth for them, what nurtured its expression, and what reinforced its presence in their workplace.

We used a simple question to elicit responses. We came to call it the *150-percent question.* Here it is: "Think of a job or project that brought out 150 percent of your energy and commitment, where you were fully engaged, when your performance was at its peak, and you found the greatest satisfaction in your work. Then identify what was it that brought out that 150 percent for you?"

Over time, we developed a framework to help people explore the 150-percent question. We asked them to think of what was true of the role they played, of the team and people they worked with, of the outcome of their work, and of its connection to their own values. You may want to explore these questions for yourself. Your answers will provide the foundation for building a Corporate Soul strategy.

The Four Paths to Corporate Soul

As we collected more and more stories, a pattern began to emerge, and we discovered that people awaken Corporate Soul via four paths. We introduce them here to provide an overview of what we learned; they will be discussed in greater detail throughout the book.

The first of the four paths we call the *Path of Self.* Soul awakens when people are aware of their own passion, in touch with their core values, and when they actively bring these alive in their daily work. Although this path is primarily about the individual discovery of vocation, leaders are responsible for developing a climate that fosters the kind of self-discovery required to be sure people bring their values and passion into the workplace.

Next is the *Path of Contribution.* In walking this path, people discover the deeper reason for their work. The value and meaning of their contribution comes alive as people recognize their daily efforts serve a worthy goal. When people see the ultimate outcome of their work as valuable, especially when it was connected to a form of service to others, soul and commitment were present as well.

Third, soul is awakened by following the *Path of Craft,* which is developing an intense enjoyment in the moment to moment action of work. Craft focuses on the ongoing process of learning and mastery that turns even the most mundane task into an artistic meditation. People reported they came alive when they were engaged in activities that called forth the highest levels of skill and made them aware of previously unknown capabilities.

Finally, there is the *Path of Community.* People find soul when their connection to others goes deeper than their job description, touches the heart, and transcends traditional team building. Through the Path of Community individuals join together to bring out the best in each other. As community members we see each others limits without blaming and call forth each others riches without demanding.

Paths Not Roads

As we began our own journey toward Corporate Soul, we had hoped to find roads that would lead us to our destination. But roads—well-defined and well-established routes—to Corporate Soul do not exist. Roads are almost always built where there were once paths. And paths evolve from the imprint of thousands of feet following the same direction. Between the modern corporation and the awakened Corporate Soul there is no efficient, black-topped road. Too few have gone far enough on this quest to provide us with a certain road to follow. Instead, a few brave pioneers have beaten tentative paths that invite further exploration.

Bringing soul to work is a task for pioneers. Hence, this book is not the definitive guidebook; it does not provide a prescription. We simply want to point the way to the paths that have worked for us and our clients, and we invite your active participation in deepening those paths so that roads may be laid in the future.

Although the specific twists and turns of each person's and each organization's path are impossible to predict, these four Paths to Corporate Soul provide a useful framework for leaders and companies to ask important questions about creating soul and commitment in our work. Lao Tsu described the process of following the paths to soul when he wrote, "There are ways, but the Great Way is uncharted."

Expect Detours

Traveling on the paths to soul can lead to many detours and seemingly wrong turns. Yet if we are paying attention, the very detours become the path. When John was working on his doctorate at Kent State University in Ohio, he took the same road every day for the one-hour drive from his home to the campus. It was an uninteresting route but familiar, quick, and easy. One day, he ran into a road-closed sign. Construction was underway and a sequence of signs led him to a detour that followed a winding and time-consuming route. After about five miles, the road turned a corner. There, sparkling in autumn splendor was a tranquil pond, reflecting the surrounding trees. John began to take this route to campus each day. He observed the pond through the senses—the autumn colors gave way to an icy white stillness, then to springtime's brilliant green. The detour had opened a new direction that became his road.

So it has been with our search for soul at work. We have taken some detours, found trails closed to us, and sometimes wondered if we would ever arrive. We are not unique in discovering that the paths we least expected would take us home with a beauty we could never have planned. As we move to an examination of each of the four paths, we recall the words of poet Antonio Machado, "Travelers, there is no path, paths are made by walking."

Anxious as one may be to get started, the traditions have always spoken about the need for preparation. There is almost always a desert experience that precedes a journey. That is why, before exploring the paths and describing the actions that lead to Corporate Soul, we turn to a discussion of what leaders can do to be sure they are prepared to walk the paths successfully.

Exercise: Reflection: Language & Business

Begin by recognizing how the words and language one uses fence out the soul. A mix of words follow. How often are these words used by you and by those in your organization?

Mark each word:

1 = rarely
2 = sometimes
3 = frequently

___ accountability
___ alignment
___ bottom line
___ community
___ compassion
___ contribution
___ efficiency
___ family-friendly
___ feeling
___ heart
___ intuition
___ joy
___ love
___ logic
___ marching orders

___ mastery
___ passion
___ people
___ performance
___ profits
___ purpose
___ responsibility
___ return on
      investment
___ service
___ shared values
___ teamwork
___ truth
___ values
___ vocation

What would it mean to include some of the rarely spoken words? Which words above are soul-awakening words?

Exercise: The 150-Percent Question

Think of a job or project you have been involved in that brought out 150 percent of your energy—a time when you felt fully engaged at work and felt you were at your best and wanted to be doing the work you were doing. What was it that brought out that 150 percent?

Some questions that will help your exploration are listed as follows:

- How did this experience connect with your personal values/passion?
- Why was outcome of the work important to you and the team?
- What kind of tasks did you perform?
- What characterized the interpersonal relationships and team dynamics?

Some Ways to Use the 150-Percent Question

- Live with this question for a few weeks identifying key times when you were able to be fully engaged at work. Then try to determine how you can bring more of those factors into your present work and job.
- Use the question as a team. Share your answers. Then identify common themes. Discuss how the team can bring more of those 150-percent factors into its current work.

"Wherever you are is the entry point."
—KABIR

"With sufficient depth, spring will
amply supply the stream." —ZEN SAYING

3

Preparing for the Journey

A friend's ex-wife was a compulsive list maker and worrier, traits he disliked in her. Whenever they took a trip, she made detailed lists of what had to be done to prepare for the trip— clothes to pack, notices to be given, things that had to be done to ensure that nothing could be left behind or undone. As much as he cursed the lists, he confided privately that his wife's preparation had paid off many times over the years.

The wisdom traditions often remind us of the importance of preparation and of the need to cleanse our inner world before we forge out to make changes in the outer world. Jesus went to the desert before beginning his mission. The Hebrews of the Old Testament wandered in the desert for forty years before entering the promised land. The Buddha went into the forest and experienced many trials before the night when he sat beneath the Bo tree and attained full enlightenment. The pattern is consistent from tradition to tradition—until the mind and heart are prepared, action is premature.

A successful journey is based on wise and thorough preparation. In beginning the journey along the Paths to Corporate Soul, it is helpful to consider how to prepare personally and organizationally. Certain attitudes and attributes should be cultivated at the outset so that the paths do not become dead ends but rather lead to the commitment that can fuel organizational renewal.

Everything Begins With Attention

The first stage of preparation for the journey is simple but essential. It is beautifully illustrated by the following Zen story.

One day a man approached Ikkyu asking, "Master, please write me a maxim of the highest wisdom." Ikkyu took his brush and wrote the word "attention."

"Is that all?" asked the man. Ikkyu then wrote "attention, attention."

"Well," said the man, "I really don't see much depth in what you have written. Is there no more?" Ikkyu wrote the word a third time.

Frustrated, the man demanded, "What does 'attention' mean anyway?"

Ikkyu responded, "Attention means attention."

Corporations have not paid much attention to the soul at work. What we pay attention to grows. Is it any wonder, then, the soul has withered in most organizations? How many companies have you heard of that have a soul strategy? In most organizations an executive would be laughed under the table for making such a suggestion. An honest self-assessment reveals that most of us have not developed a soul strategy for ourselves either. But without a strategy, or at least a consistent practice, it is difficult to bring about any meaningful soul development. Strategies and practices do not appear out of nowhere. They require attention.

It is easy to "think about" soul. But thinking about it is not the same as giving attention. Thinking about soul does not engage our total being. To think about soul is to be entertained or distracted from one's everyday struggles. Thinking about soul is a noncommittal way of proceeding. "I'll think about it," we tell ourselves and then let the matter drop. Giving attention to soul is more challenging and more demanding; it takes a deeper, more complete investment. Runners who are training for a race give their attention to running in a way that changes them and prepares them for the race. Those who merely think about running remain arm chair athletes.

Our professed value of integrating soul and spirituality into our work was out of alignment with our actual behavior. This mismatch was not based on a lack of thinking about the subject. In fact, we talked about it so much, our conversations became a substitute for investing ourselves and making the deeper changes necessary to really get started. As you prepare to explore the Four Paths to Corporate Soul, stop and ask yourself if you are ready to move from thinking about soul to giving attention—investing the time, resources, and energy the soul requires to come alive. We made the shift from thinking about the soul of our work to giving true attention over the last few years.

Becoming the Right Person: Shedding the Victim Mindset

We have noticed a curious phenomenon in our seminars and consulting work over the last decade. Although we have conducted sessions with literally hundreds of groups, the right people have never once been in the room. When we conduct sessions with frontline employees, they say, "This is great and if the managers would just get it, we could do something." When we meet with senior executives, they say, "The middle folks don't get it; we do." The middle folks lament both those above and below. Who are the right people?

In addition, preparing for the journey of soul means taking responsibility for awakening our own soul and creating an environment that calls forth soul from our colleagues. In the Zen tradition, it is said, "Wherever you are, you are the master." The master is the one who realizes the only way to influence the future is to become the "right person" in the present moment. From this awareness comes soulful leadership action. To be this kind of master is to recognize oneself as the "right person," the person who chooses to create something of value rather than wait for others to take initiative. Being the master does not mean people will magically fall in line and start obeying you. It means that one stops waiting for a miracle to happen and instead chooses to move forward and create the conditions that awaken soul. To become the master is to become inspired by one's core values and to take actions that align with those values. By contrast, passive waiting is the breeding ground of resentment and cynicism. It produces a defeatist inversion of the Zen statement, "Wherever I am, I am a victim."

Powerlessness is a mindset that can touch any level in the organizational hierarchy. A CEO at one of the largest health care companies in the world said shortly after getting the job, "People think I have magic buttons in my office. I just wish once I could find one of them and that when I pushed it something would happen!" Powerlessness distracts us from choosing to be the "right person" and focuses us on what others are doing.

Time magazine ran a cover story describing the "victim-mentality that permeates the United States." In this mindset everything that goes wrong is someone else's fault. Such attitudes have a familiar ring to many in the corporate world where many, even those at the top, believe someone else must make the first move if soul is to take flight within the company.

During seminars, we frequently ask people how they know when they are stuck in the victim trap. They tell us it is when they start saying things such as, "We didn't do it," "It's not our fault," "If it weren't for them...," "If they would just change...."

Awakening Corporate Soul is a full participation sport. Ask yourself whether you are approaching the journey to Corporate Soul as a master or as a victim. Have you started to think about what you can do to awaken a soul in your own career and for the larger organization? Or are you coming up with ideas that require someone else to give you permission before they can be implemented?

Personal responsibility is essential if real changes are to be made. Victims do nothing but feel coerced by changes others initiate. Sadly, organizational hierarchies have fostered an obedience mentality that is too passive to deal with the fundamental changes that are required in times of rapid transition. Recognizing this habit of passivity in oneself and others is part of preparing for the journey. Then choosing a new attitude, a new belief—"Wherever I am, I am the master"—moves the action forward.

Helping People Take Responsibility for Soul at Work

Leaders can help people take responsibility in many ways. One of the simplest is to let people know when they are falling into victim behavior or victim language. By reflecting what one sees and hears in a nonblaming and compassionate way, leaders can support others to choose responsibility.

A consultant colleague, Linda, was working with managers at a public utility on strategies for managing change. "Nothing will change," announced one manager who had been with the organization for a dozen years. All morning he repeated his conclusion that nothing could or would change. He had also mentioned while introducing himself to the group that over the years he and his wife had cared for many foster children.

At the first break Linda went right over to the manager and engaged him in a conversation about his experience as a foster parent. She asked if the children came to him with a sense of hope.

"No," he said, "they have pretty much given up. So the first thing you have to do is help them see that it can be different and that they are part of making it different."

Linda pointed out that the same was true in his organization. Although there was reason for skepticism, change would not be possible until there was hope. Corporate Soul is not easily attained. A culture of awakened commitment is the by-product of years of focus and attention. Getting everyone within a corporation to be willing to look inside themselves, rid themselves of outmoded habits, and openly explore new choices is not finished in a two-day workshop. Awakening soul is a long-term commitment.

Living With Soul Questions

The power of the well-designed question to turn us inside out is well recognized in the wisdom traditions. The right question at the right time can function as a spiritual catalyst. Questions become doorways that open us to new domains of choice previously unconsidered. In the Zen tradition the use of such provocative and awakening questions—called *koans*—has been developed to a fine art. Used as part of Zen training, these *koans,* often posed in riddle-like phrases, act as catalysts to initiate breakthroughs in thinking, perceiving, and acting.

A well-known example of a *koan* asks, "What is the sound of one hand clapping?" Through concentration and meditation, the Zen student seeks to break through the apparently insoluble nature of this question. Thinking about the *koan* is useless for a *koan* is a spiritual tool, not an intellectual puzzle. The Zen student is not wrestling so much with the *koan* as with his or her own mind and life. By an investment of total attention, the Zen student grasps the "answer" to the *koan* and in so doing solves the riddle of his or her life.

Koans are not reserved for the followers of Zen. Each of us has burning life and work questions that seem, on the surface, impossible to answer. We call these questions personal *koans.* Examples of personal *koans* include, "How can I bring more meaning into my work?" "Is this what I am meant to do?" "Is there room for the soul in this workplace?" Intellectual answers to personal *koans* are beside the point. The purpose of such questions is to bring us face-to-face with our life and work. Our personal *koans* act as mirrors in which we see whether we have made our life and work hospitable to the soul within us.

One of the most important aspects of preparation for the journey to Corporate Soul is the identification of one's personal *koans.* It is important to emphasize that you already have one or more personal *koans.* You will hear these primary, soulful questions repeating themselves. Some of these questions appear in those in-between times—during the drive home or waiting for the elevator to open. Many find such questions staring back at them when they awaken in the middle of the night. Try listening to yourself when you talk with a close friend, or when your mind ruminates on a slow commute. Listen to your internal dialogue after a particularly frustrating day or meeting. If you listen to your thoughts for a few days, you will hear these primary, soulful questions whispering.

Answering a personal *koan* is an act of living not thinking. When Gandhi was asked, "What is your message?" he replied, "My life is my message." The way we live and work is the expression of our soul. Honestly asking a personal *koan* means actively living with a burning question in daily work and life. Answering a personal *koan* is an act of courage. For answering a life-changing question means changing one's life.

In his preparation to awaken soul at work, John identified three personal *koans* to use on a daily basis:

1. What ignites my passion and commitment in today's work?
2. How can I bring more soul to this moment?
3. What would I like my legacy to be in this assignment?

John asked the first question in the morning as he reviewed his daily schedule and to-do list. With the personal *koan* as a filter he could link the completion of his daily tasks to the awakening of his soul. Meeting outer responsibilities and fulfilling inner goals became one process. Using this first question enabled John to reclaim his attention from the tyranny of the urgent and redirect it toward what was truly valuable.

The second *koan* was used throughout the day as appropriate. This question became a favorite of both of ours for the way it changed our way of viewing often difficult situations. We found that whenever we were stuck in a disagreement or going in circles in a conversation by asking ourselves how we could "bring more soul to this moment," we would seem to magically disengage ourselves from the emotional entanglement that was developing. Then with a fresh inner perspective, we could address the issue or the person in a more constructive manner.

The third *koan* was used whenever a project or work assignment began to weigh heavily on the soul. Rather than become a victim of work pressures, by using this question, we would see how to bring more value and meaning to an onerous process.

Corporate *Koans*

Koans are not just personal. Groups, teams, and organizations have their own burning and potentially transformative questions. We call these the corporate *koans.* Corporate *koans* are the questions that need to be addressed collectively if an organization is to move into new levels of service, performance, and community. More than with personal *koans,* there can be a tremendous amount of fear about verbalizing these questions. They feel too big, too impossible, to be put on the table. Often such corporate *koans* are spoken only behind closed doors. Yet when brought forth and lived with, corporate *koans* focus collective attention and catalyze collective action.

It takes tremendous mental, emotional, and spiritual energy to transform an organization. Finding and asking the right questions is an elegant way to move the corporate mountain. This is how leaders can spark deeper levels of awareness and change in the organization. Not by making grand pronouncements but simply by posing powerful questions. When an organization is gripped by a potent question it begins to move. What corporate *koans* would you like to be on the mind's of the people in your organization?

Examples of such corporate *koans* include, but are certainly not limited to, the following:

- What brings meaning and community to our company?
- How can this meeting or project be an expression of our highest aims?
- What would be of service right now?
- How can this conversation be more open, clear, or authentic?
- What is our larger responsibility as a team or organization?

Years ago we attended a talk about the stages of the human life cycle. In discussing mid-life, the speaker said, "It does not much matter how you answer the questions of mid-life; it is the asking that is essential!"

The same can be said of personal and corporate *koans*. Until they are asked, the answers will not be lived.

Speaking the Truth

The willingness to speak the truth and the desire to create a climate in which the truth can be spoken are essential to awakening Corporate Soul. For many people, the most devitalizing aspect of organizational life is the sheer lack of truth-telling that goes on within the corporate walls. It is easy to recall times when there was something you had to say but said nothing, or when you wanted to say something far more honest than what actually came out of your mouth. You've seen the same pattern in others. The willingness to speak our truth and to allow others to speak their truth is a prerequisite of the high commitment workplace.

Spiritual traditions are filled with stories pointing to our need to speak the truth. One of our favorites is that of the prodigal son from the New Testament. In this story, a rich young man desires to leave home to explore his own life. The youth asks his father for an advance on his inheritance and goes his own way. He squanders his wealth frivolously and is reduced to cleaning up after swine at another man's farm to eke out a pathetic income.

Metaphorically, this story reflects the experience of many at work. People enter the working world seeking to explore and discover our own life. Instead, we find that our resources—creativity, caring, enthusiasm, idealism—have been squandered. Or perhaps they find themselves in a soul stifling workplace where commitment and purpose never rise above lukewarm. One may complain about a soul-starving situation but complaining is not the same as truth-telling. Some may even lie to themselves pretending nothing more is wanted or expected from work. Many find themselves living in this state for years.

In the story of the prodigal son, there is a moment of awakening in which the young man says to himself, "Do not even my father's servants eat better than this?" Asking this question was an act of truth-telling. Before this moment the young man may have sensed the truth but did not articulate it. Unspoken truth has no power to generate action. By speaking the truth, the prodigal son is propelled onto the path that leads back home.

The story turns on this central point—until we admit to ourselves that we want more, more is not possible.

Often, the consequence of speaking truth openly to oneself, let alone to anyone else, is simply too threatening. Janet, a former vice president of a large bank, told us this in retrospect: "For years I knew my soul was dying but admitting that to myself and leaving the security of my hard-earned position was more than I could do!" Speaking the truth makes change possible.

The Power of Corporate Truth-Telling

In the corporate setting, conventional wisdom has it that telling the truth is a sure way of getting into deep water and that the political consequences of challenging the status quo will bring the walls of the organization down on the person who finds his or her voice. To be sure, this happens, but most often when people speak the truth, they are expressing the thoughts and feelings of others within the organization. Their personal courage to speak opens a door for others. One work can be the beginning of a collective journey.

Donna, a middle manager at a biotech firm spoke up at a manager's meeting. She said the company had become a desert. "All sense of purpose, energy, and commitment had dried up within the organization," Donna said, even while fearing retribution. She spoke out in a public forum, uncertain if her colleagues, who privately had agreed with her, would openly lend their support. "I thought I might end up being a voice crying out in the wilderness just before I was executed," she confessed. But her words struck a chord.

Other voices from colleagues and senior executives rose up in a chorus with hers. From her words, a year-long process of renewal began.

A frontline worker in the semiconductor industry spoke her truth in a meeting that had degenerated into a ritual of endless complaining against the company from her victim-minded colleagues. In a moment of exasperation she dared to say, "Yes, there are problems, and as if that were not enough, I have to come in here everyday and listen to you folks complain all day long!" Tough talk, but it broke the mood and opened up the possibility for others to admit their own frustration with what one person called the "daily moaning and groaning."

Complaining about conditions is a distorted kind of truth-telling. It gets at the problems but depletes any energy for change. Complaining tells only the victim's truth: "Things are bad and there is nothing I can do," which is a useless and deadening perspective on life and work. Truth-telling that does not catalyze productive action is not soulful truth. Truth-telling that awakens the soul calls forth the energy of change.

In the corporate setting telling the truth will sometimes get you branded a rebel, a malcontent, a disloyal soldier. Yet it is difficult to imagine soul emerging for most of us without some truth-telling along the way. Leadership demands the courage to create an environment that allows for, even encourages, the truth. Such candor may be unnerving at first, but soul cannot emerge without this creative tension.

Leadership demands the courage to create an environment that allows for, even encourages, the truth. The CEO of a new 18,000-person organization had called an off-site meeting of the top hundred managers. We were facilitating the process which included an examination of the past twelve-month start-up phase. Not surprisingly, the organization had been living through a period of chaos. People had been working long hours—sacrificing their evenings and weekends—to ensure the birth of the new company. The mantra on everyone's lips was, "I have no life and I am losing my family!"

What does a leader say in such a situation? This CEO stood up and spoke from the heart. "We need to move away from the kind of culture we have fallen into," he told his managers. "I do not want to perpetuate an environment in which our personal lives are sacrificed to meet corporate goals." He spoke of his desire to create an organization that honored the need for balance not just achievement. "But my saying this is not enough. Everyone of us must be willing to push back when the demands get out of hand. We have to be willing to talk about the ways in which we are sacrificing ourselves and to tell the truth about what is happening to us. Only then, can we begin the process of change."

Such candor may be unnerving at first, but soul cannot awaken without the challenging presence of the truth.

Moving From the Desert

It is tempting in these days of quick prescriptions and "ten easy steps" to try and start the journey to Corporate Soul without being prepared. The Four Paths that follow can awaken Corporate Soul but only in companies and among leaders who have the four essentials for soulful travelers:

1. Giving attention to the soul and not just thinking about it
2. Taking self-responsibility for renewal and shedding the victim "mindset"
3. Living the real questions (personal and corporate *koans)*
4. Speaking and listening to the truth

Preparation is essential to creating the kind of company that can succeed in turbulent times. A Chinese proverb advises, "Wait long, strike fast." It is by investing time in preparation that we make it possible to complete our journey.

Exercise: Preparing for the Journey

Attention and Reflection

1. How much attention are you paying to fostering more soul in your own work? (Attention refers to time for deliberation and action.)
2. How about your company?
3. What could you do immediately to pay more attention to fostering soul in your organization?

Speaking the Truth

1. How are you doing at speaking the truth to yourself and to others about your work and workplace?
2. Have you fostered a company where the truth can be spoken?
3. What could be done to encourage productive truth-telling in your organization?

Taking Responsibility—Becoming the Right Person

1. How are you doing at taking responsibility for creating soul and commitment in your own work?
2. Do you find yourself in a victim mindset about your work or company? If so, how can you begin to break this pattern?
3. Is your organization pervaded with a sense of victim thinking?

Exercise: What Are Your Personal *Koans?*

Identifying your personal koans provides a focus
that shifts one's attention from the superficial to
the essential. Personal *koans* are the transforming
guides that lead us forward on the Paths to
Corporate Soul. What questions do you want to ask
about your work or workplace? Write them down. If
some sound cliché, don't judge yourself. Most of
the deepest questions have been asked thousands of
times before. That doesn't disqualify them as
personally relevant.

_____
_____
_____
_____
_____
_____
_____
_____
_____
_____
_____
_____
_____

Exercise: A Truth You Must Tell

What is a truth you must tell to yourself about your present work or workplace.

_____
_____
_____
_____

What is the implication(s) of this truth for you personally? What does it tell you must be done? Discussed with others? Planned for?

_____
_____
_____
_____
_____
_____
_____
_____

Identify a truth that must be told within your company.

_____
_____
_____
_____
_____
_____
_____
_____

To whom can you safely tell this?

_____

_____

_____

_____

_____

_____

Who will be more challenging to tell but must hear this truth?

_____

_____

_____

_____

_____

_____

_____

What conversation will you initiate in the near future? (Give yourself a time frame.)

_____

_____

_____

_____

_____

_____

"A human being has so many skins inside, covering the
depths of the heart. We know so many things,
but we do not know ourselves."
—Meister Eckhart

If you bring forth what is within you
what you bring forth will save you.
If you do not bring forth what is within you
what you do not bring forth will destroy you.
—Gospel of Thomas

4

The Path of Self:
Why Personal Passion Is Critical

There is a picture in Eric's photo album of him running around the playground in New York's Central Park dressed in full cowboy regalia—red shirt with ivory buttons, bandanna, full-brimmed hat, jeans, boots, engraved belt, holster, gun, and the thing that brought it all together—chaps. The spitting image of a cowboy. And, in his five-year-old heart, a true one.

At every stage of life the question, "Who am I?" reasserts itself. And at every stage of life we try to answer. In childhood there is great freedom to our response; in a single hour a child answers this core question a dozen times, transforming from chef to super hero to eagle. As an adolescent our response takes on more intensity—every movement of the body, every hair (or shaved skull) declares one's identity. As an adult the question of identity continues but often in the background. The demands of daily life, the pressures of deadlines, and the clamoring chorus of responsibilities often drown out any inner questing. But the question remains, manifesting itself for many as the form of a mid-life course correction aimed at avoiding the death of the inner self before it is too late. Like a radical medical treatment, such crisis interventions have their own side effects, which are often quite traumatic.

As we interviewed people about soul at work, the first of the four paths that emerged was the *Path of Self*. We discovered that when people know their own passions, when their work is an outgrowth of that passion, and when their personal values live through their work— energy flows and commitment grows.

Mirror, Mirror On the Wall

Each morning as we look in the mirror, whether we are aware of it or not, there is a part of us that asks, "Who am I? Is the work I will do today truly my passion or someone else's agenda I am blindly pursuing? Can I be myself today at work or will I have to don a mask and play to the audience of my colleagues and customers?"

Although the term "putting on my face" usually refers to cosmetics, the fact is, we all prepare ourselves to meet the world. This is not an issue of makeup but of inner orientation. The time we take in front of the mirror is as much about recognizing ourselves as it is preparing the face we will present to the world. The glossiest lipstick can reveal as much as it can conceal.

Who Is That Masked Man?

In the ancient Greek theater every character was recognizable by the mask worn. The mask revealed the character's persona—their role in the drama. The mask was the character's identity. Today, the term persona still means mask, but it has taken on the connotation of "masking" in the sense of hiding, or disguising something rather than pointing to something authentic. The term persona now refers most often to a socially constructed self, adapted to the demands of the outer world, not the deeper more authentic self we feel to be our essence.

This raises a question for those who would awaken Corporate Soul: Can we stay competitive with an organization of personas? Can a persona-based workforce generate the commitment or creativity required to maintain market share in today's pressured economy?

When facing a project deadline, a departmental crisis, a new competitive threat, or a problematic budget issue, the question, "Who am I?" may appear more suited to a coffee house on a college campus than to the corridors of a corporation. When wearing the leader "hat" one may wonder if this question has any relevance to the need to be competitive and profitable. "I don't have time for navel gazing" is our pragmatic response. Yet, if we are to awaken the Corporate Soul and infuse our work life with deep, sustainable human energy, there is no other place to start than with the quest for the authentic self, the inner core that Meister Eckhart called the divine spark within.

At a seminar for sales professionals a woman stood up and shared her story. She told the group that "being a salesperson was never my dream. I wanted to be a teacher. Sales was my sister's passion." She found herself seventeen years later burned out and disappointed, unable to fire up her enthusiasm for work that was never her passion. Her inner spark was flickering out.

Imagine an entire organization filled with people who are living someone else's passion. Imagine an organization where few people know what kind of work calls forth their highest commitment. Then imagine the opposite. Where do you want to work? Which environment would attract people with whom you want to work? In which organization would there be energy and commitment?

Companies and leaders must be interested in awakening the person behind the mask and in helping people recover their true passion. An organization full of people plying other's passions cannot maintain peak performance. What's more, the courage to explore the fit between inner self or soul and work is a prerequisite to an awakened Corporate Soul.

In our interviews regarding soul at work, people say that they are most committed when their work is a true expression of who they are—of their inner selves, an expression of their values and personal vision. For those pursuing the Corporate Soul, the questions each morning remain: Am I bringing my authentic self to work or just my persona? As I work, am I in contact with the Corporate Soul or with the Corporate Mask?

By following the Path of Self people become aware of their own passion and touch their deeper values. Although this Path is by definition personal, leaders have a hand in developing the kind of climate that fosters self discovery and engages people's deepest energies in their work. Leaders can help unleash commitment or can reinforce the shallow level of engagement that the persona can give.

Uncovering Masks at Work

A Hasidic story deals with the issue of masks and self. It is said that in the eastern European town of Minsk there lived a great tailor named Rubleman. The suits he crafted were not only exquisite but also quite expensive. They were the sartorial symbol of success. In the same town there lived a young man, Stern, whose life was characterized by hard times and difficulties. Nothing seemed to work out for Stern, so he decided to leave Minsk and seek improved fortunes elsewhere.

Many years later, Stern became quite prosperous. He decided to return to Minsk and purchase a suit from Rubleman so he could parade his wealth before his former townsfolk. Arriving in Minsk, he went to the great tailor's shop to demand the best possible suit money could buy. Rubleman brought out a garment of the finest weave. The colors and texture were outstanding. Unfortunately, when Stern tried it on, he found one arm was too long, one leg was too short, and the shoulders were cut in a strange asymmetrical pattern.

"Do not worry," said the tailor. "Simply bend forward like this." He guided Stern into an awkward, contorted position—half stooping forward, standing on the toe of one foot, and with one arm crooked at a right angle. Stern's shoulders, although aching from the position he held, molded perfectly with the suit's asymmetrical cut. Stepping back to determine the results of his adjustments, Rubleman smiled. Stern paid for the suit and limped out of the shop maintaining his contorted posture. Halfway down the street two elderly women paused to watch him. "That poor man," said one.

"Yes, but look at how beautifully the suit fits him," remarked the other.

This tale humorously illustrates the dilemma of many in the modern corporation. We have twisted and contorted ourselves into the parameters of the "suit" while ignoring the more natural requirements of our own natures. In an attempt to be successful within the corporate structure, we have often bent ourselves out of shape. We have found a way of making the outer suit fit but often at the expense of the inner spark. Because we are uncomfortable and so much of our energy is spent maintaining a contorted position, we lose touch with many of our natural desires and abilities. The energy that could be channeled creatively is bound up in maintaining a position.

Walking the Path of Self means asking oneself—Where am I wearing a Rubleman suit? In what work situation, work relationship, and so on, have I twisted myself in such a way that it is fundamentally uncomfortable and unnatural? What are the costs of this contortion to myself and to the organization?

Ramana Maharishi, one of modern India's greatest saints, tutored those who came for spiritual guidance to inquire deeply into the question, "Who am I?" If we truly penetrate that question, he promised, all illusions, all masks, would fall away. This simple question is the flint that can rekindle true commitment. Those individuals who have found time to inquire into their true identities have found a path of inquiry that leads away from reactionary thinking toward a sustainable source of creativity and commitment.

The first steps toward the Corporate Soul are profitably spent by granting time, space, and legitimacy to the kinds of primal inquiries that have fallen out of favor in the fast-forward race most of us call work. This path begins with the question, "Who am I?" In fact, when we consciously enter the Path of Self, the contrast between our natural, inner nature and the Rubleman suit we wear each day can be almost comical (or tragic, depending on your perspective).

Grappling With the Soul Questions

The Path of Self is not an intellectual puzzle. "Who am I?" is not a question from some cosmic SAT test. To the degree our inquiry into self is a mental exercise to that degree will the soul remain out of reach. Like all truly soulful questions, "Who am I?" requires a full-bodied response. This question most often makes itself known in the form of life conditions that force us to examine whether we are expressing or distorting our deepest values.

Consider how Eric, a yoga priest and meditation teacher, could resolve the dichotomy between his spiritual values and his employment at one of the nation's largest defense contractors. One might wonder—Should he have worked there at all? For Eric, there were no easy answers to this question. As a yogi, father, husband, and management trainer, Eric found himself trying to balance many forces. His financial responsibilities, his career aspirations, and his spiritual dreams all vied for his undivided attention. Taken one at a time each of these forces represented a useful, positive aspect of Eric's nature. But when taken together these aspects did not mesh harmoniously. He felt torn between valid yet competing life directions.

Such tensions are hardly the sole property of yogis, priests, or meditators. For many, the soul makes itself known in the form of competing and seemingly unresolvable choices—the uneasy balance between work and family, the tension between keeping busy and taking care of one's own health, the pull between security and adventure.

It may seem strange for soul to appear in the midst of tensions. There is a romantic hope that following the Path of Self will be one blissful moment after another. Having chosen to awaken our soul we expect enlightenment to arrive in a stretch limo—the drinks are iced and the music is playing as we proceed to our perfect destination on a cushion of air. In stark contrast to this fantasy, the actual Path of Self is unpaved, rocky, and follows an often strenuous route. It is through our tensions that the soul first becomes known. Then it is through resolving these tensions that the powers of the soul are released. Awakening the soul is tough, honest work.

There is a part in us all that would prefer to wait for the "spiritual" stretch limo than work with our legitimate soul-filled tensions. Many try to "handle" their inner tensions through time management techniques—and look to their organizer for help. "If I can just manage my time more efficiently," the thought goes, "I will be able to handle all these competing demands." Quick and easy techniques for making fundamental tensions disappear rarely work. Why? Because these tensions are not problems to be solved but signs to follow.

Specifically, they are signposts on the Path of Self that point us toward new attitudes: "Either my work is an expression of soul or it is a sellout." This attitude is too one-sided to make room for the richness of the Soul. Either-or thinking cannot release the soul energies that are bound up in our tensions and our questions. Attempting to solve our deepest questions through either-or thinking perpetuates our spiritual crisis, which was born from just such thinking in the first place.

After fruitlessly trying to "solve" the problem of competing tensions, many just decide to "be realistic." Then, caught in the net of their own unresolvable contradictions these "realists" fall into a state of complaining cynicism. Some get tough and reject any hints that there may be an inner spark. Others point an accusing finger at the organization as if the job and not themselves held the possibility of bringing soul to their daily efforts.

One of the prerequisites for pursuing the Path of Self is to take responsibility for the soulfulness, the sense of aliveness, in our work. As a spiritual discipline, walking the Path of Self means we accept primary responsibility for our sense of fulfillment.

Sure, we can end up at the "wrong" job. But when we understand this very "wrongness" to be a powerful wake-up call that is shaking us out of our lethargy and telling us to make work more congruent with our talents and values—then *wrong* becomes *right*. A former physician, now working in a high-tech firm, told us,

"Finally, it dawned on me that my unhappiness at the hospital was seeping into every aspect of my life—my marriage, my kids, my health. Seeing that I had let things get that out of balance wasn't pretty. It was a wake-up call to change what I was doing." For some resolving their inner contradictions may mean changing careers. For most it means changing the way they think and act in their current work. By seeing work in a new way it is possible to bring the soul's values to bear on the situation at hand.

For Eric all this meant not rushing into a simple but superficial answer to his job dilemma. It meant living in the tension of being half-in and half-out of his own Rubleman suit. It meant taking responsibility for bringing more and more of his deeper values into the workplace while seeking a more compatible venue in which to awaken Corporate Soul.

Resolving primary tensions and unleashing soul power is fundamental to this Path of Self. It is a practice grounded in patience and self awareness. When we discover that we are stuck in a Rubleman suit the tendency is to try and immediately throw off our jacket. Then, feeling naked, we tend to put it right back on. Emotionally alternating between anger and fear we end up frustrated. We wonder if there are answers to our seemingly unresolvable tensions. The wisdom traditions tell us that answers to our deepest questions come at unexpected hours. They cannot be forced or fabricated. Henry David Thoreau wrote, "Only that day dawns to which you are awake." Answers do come but if we are asleep, cynical, or discouraged, they may pass us unnoticed.

The Unknown Passion

Rabbi Zashu told his students, "When I die, God will not ask me was I like Moses or was I like Joshua in my life. He will ask me, was I Zashu." We needn't wait for physical death to answer our soul questions.

Many do not even know if their work is their passion. Our friend Marc works with senior managers who have been laid off, helping them to gain reemployment and clarity regarding their chosen direction. "Many executives come to me in a state of confusion," he told us. "They are upset about having been displaced, but at the same time many do not want to go back to the same type of situation. Yet, for most, the very question, 'What do you want?' draws a huge blank."

"I focused on perfecting my performance," a woman who was vice president in a major consumer products firm told us. "That was what was required and rewarded. If I wanted to advance my career it seemed necessary to set many of my own needs aside. Basically, I stopped listening to my inner voice. Now, if I want to keep doing this work I have to start listening. If I don't, I know I won't last. Too much of 'me' is left out of what I'm doing."

This manager's realization echoes the words of Rumi: "There is a light seed grain inside. You fill it with yourself, or it dies."

Stillness and Soul

Exploring the Path of Self begins by moving from activity to stillness—alien territory for most companies. Moving toward stillness means taking time out from the "real" work to focus inwardly. For leaders it means carving time out of the schedule for people to reflect on what they truly want their work to be about? What the values are by which they wish to guide their work life? What legacy would they like to leave behind in the company and in their careers? What is their passion and how can more of it be brought to the present job?

It is only in stillness and inner quietness that we can hear what has been called the *still small voice* of the soul. This voice speaks simply and directly about what is really important. Most of the time our ears and minds are filled with the blaring trumpets and pounding drums of our desires and fears. The noise drowns out the voice of the soul. When there is no time for stillness we drift into surface living, our choices governed more by reactive emotions than creative soul prompting.

What does it mean for a company to create an environment of inner listening? Several organizations have formed career development programs which encourage reflection via a series of self-discovery questions such as Who am I? What do I value? What is my passion at work? How can more of these be present in my current job and in our team?

Such efforts support individual responsibility for identifying one's values and passions at work and to take actions to incorporate these into one's daily work. In our experience with programs of this type, employees at all levels come alive, especially since many of them have rarely taken the time to answer these critical issues on their own.

Of course, it could be argued that such efforts have too tenuous a connection to the profit margin to be worthy of investment. It could also be argued that companies have no right to have people ask what are essentially very personal and private questions. While both arguments have face validity, an organization filled with personas, with people working at other people's passions, or waiting for someone else to take actions to empower them will not thrive in a changing marketplace.

To make self-inquiry off-limits is shortsighted. Indeed, Tom Peters has said that corporations should not get involved in peoples' religious beliefs. We could not agree more. But there is an important difference between tinkering with religious beliefs and opening the workplace to conversations regarding the values that inspire commitment and promote personal fulfillment. The corporation should not tell people what to believe or what to value, but it has a responsibility to allow for deeply spiritual questions to be asked and answered at work in ways that promote personal and corporate integrity.

There are leaders who fear these kinds of questions. In the early days of Eric's career at a Fortune 500 corporation, he presented management training programs that included exercises in values clarification. One of the engineering managers, with a notoriously explosive personality, sent several of his key people. Shortly after the program, Eric's manager's phone was ringing. "What in the devil is that trainer up to!?" the engineering manager's hysterical voice projected through the phone lines and echoed against the walls of the training department. "We don't want these people thinking about what they want! They might think about leaving."

This manager embodied a soul-crushing attitude that replaced commitment with toe-the-line compliance.

He practiced a form of management that aspired to obedience rather than commitment. This manager espoused the fearful belief that reflective questions were devilish and could only lead to organizational destruction. He acted as though the goal of leadership was to distract people from their values because true enthusiasm was too much to expect. In fact, the opposite is true. It is the unasked questions and the unacknowledged values that sabotage commitment from within.

The workplace cannot be excluded from the search for authentic depth and vitality that is the innate urge of the soul. Too much is at stake, both personally and organizationally. Deep values never really go away. In the Gospel of Thomas, Jesus says, "If you bring forth what is within you, what you bring forth will save you. If you do not bring forth what is within you, what you do not bring forth will destroy you." If the energies of the soul do not open out into the world, they turn poisonous and inwardly destructive. When we hold our gifts, talents, and values hostage to fear or doubt these very life giving resources begin to eat away at the foundations of our sense of self. One can see this in many organizations where there are people who have forsaken themselves while remaining on the job. They become unhelpful team members, often releasing their own bitter form of "realism" in meetings and conversations.

For leaders the above quotation from the Gospel of Thomas offers particularly chilling guidance. By ignoring or repressing the powerful soul energies that lie dormant within the Corporate Soul, leaders can unintentionally create the conditions for poisonous, destructive forces to breed. The same energies that can bring about passion, commitment and productivity, will turn to cynicism, apathy, and resistance if stifled.

The Corporate Path of Self

By walking the Path of Self, personal and corporate values connect. Over the past decade, the creation of vision, mission, and values statements has become de rigueur—an indispensable ritual of corporate life. It is the rare lobby that does not display a framed vision or mission statement. Few companies believe they can live without them. A cartoon in *New Yorker* magazine reveals how deeply this ritual has penetrated the culture. A husband and wife are pictured sitting in separate chairs in their living room. The wife is speaking with her arms crossed in indignation as the husband looks at her nonplussed. "No," she says, "I don't think a mission statement will improve our marriage."

We have been part of the creation of many of these statements but have come to believe that, for the most part, such rituals in and of themselves do little to inspire corporate commitment. But vision statements can be more than platitudes. When St. Mary's Health Care began to revamp its health care delivery system, leaders determined that sustainable success hinged on employees who were committed and caring. The fiscal price of hiring and training was too high and the spiritual price of creating a hospital devoid of the spirit of compassion was too great. St. Mary's leadership met to articulate a new vision for the organization. But to do so they discovered it was necessary to examine their own beliefs and values. What could have been a perfunctory visioning session, resulting in a fiscally demanding yet spiritually safe statement such as, "Be Number One" became a deeply challenging inquiry into what this group of leaders truly wanted to create.

Visioning sessions, as important as they are in concept, can become yet another way of reinforcing masks. It is easier in most organizations to say, "Kill the competition," than to ask, "What are we really trying to create here?" Such a question jostles the mask and asks us to step out of our Rubleman suit to stand clothed only in our values. It can make us feel pretty naked and exposed to stand there in such a state. Most play it safe spiritually, even while piling on higher and higher business targets.

Few organizations allow for, let alone take time to help workers explore their own deepest values. Instead the organization's values are paraded before them and a salute of support is assumed (it often comes from an unanticipated finger). When people can start with exploring their own values and then connect those values to the organization's goals, Corporate Soul begins to awaken.

The American division of Fiat chose to create its vision statement in this way. Beginning with individual visions a process was established whereby the multitude of personal visions were discussed and integrated into a single vision that everyone recognized as "mine." By creating the vision from the bottom up, not from the top down, the organization truly rallied around a core set of shared values and goals. Telus, a Canadian telephone company, created its "corporate principles" by having people throughout the organization identify their personal values. These formed the basis for the corporate values.

The St. Mary's leaders invited each person in the organization to spend time clarifying and articulating his or her own most cherished values. Employees were then asked to discover or create ways in which they could express those values in their current work at the hospital. Finally, they were asked to identify ways in which their own values aligned with those of the company. The welling forth of emotional and intellectual energies that happened is something most mangers would be happy to buy at any price. "I am working harder than ever," said one St. Mary's employee. "Not because I have to but because this job is the place were I become more of myself."

Fasting for the Corporate Soul

The wisdom traditions have always honored fasting as a way of radically shifting ourselves from the ruts of our habits. In essence fasting is the practice of not feeding the habits of the past that limit us. Fasting withdraws our energy from the outmoded habit as we reinvest ourselves more fully in a new way of being. The most familiar form of fasting is from food—a practice not directly related to awakening Corporate Soul.

But it is possible to fast from any "thing" as well as any "behavior." We can stop feeding any limiting way of being or acting. As we walk the Path of Self it is useful to determine which behaviors are worth keeping and which worth eliminating. These become the focus of a fast.

One of Eric's coworkers recognized a tendency to indulge in caustic and sometimes sarcastic speech. This way of speaking ran counter to the values he wanted to incarnate in his work. He decided to go on a sarcasm fast. "I began very enthusiastically. I was determined never to be sarcastic again. That approach didn't work." What our friend discovered was that by practicing targeted fasting, for example by determining that during a three-hour period in the morning he would fast from sarcasm, the process became both more manageable and more successful. "It became a creative game for me," he said. "I looked forward to times of sarcasm fasting. Instead of being a heavy discipline it was fun. I enjoyed the changes that came as I became less and less sarcastic in my communication."

This process of fasting can also be applied by a group. The information systems department of a large electronics firm explored this practice at one of its team meetings. "We recognized that we were feeling victimized by one of our customers," reported a team member. "We noticed that everyone felt bad about working with this customer, complained to each other, and generally acted like we were powerless." The team chose to fast for a week from victim-based complaining about this customer and instead to look for and speak of creating a new relationship that had integrity and fulfilled their mission of service.

In a follow-up meeting the team members agreed that the fast had been a success. "Not that I was perfect," pointed out one member, "but I found that I noticed the old victim behavior as it got started and it was easier to nip in the bud." Another team member reported, "I realized that it wasn't the customer who was victimizing me, it was my own habit of thinking and talking like a victim."

What is a habit from the past that you would like to stop feeding? Is there a way of thinking or interacting that you fall into but that does not support your deeper values? What about a particular behavior pattern? Identify one that would be worth fasting from. Target the time period for the fast, and try it out.

Working With Inner Obstacles

Treading the Path of Self is a conscious investment of time and resources. As with any investment there are risks and rewards. The possible risks are that such personal inquiry will lead to little organizational benefit. The possible rewards are that people begin to bring more of their energy, creativity, and commitment to the workplace.

The Corporate Soul awakens first when the individual soul wakes up and says, in the words of Gerard Manley Hopkins, "For this was I born, for this I came into the world." To awaken the soul requires both reflection and action. An anonymous Indian poet wrote what can be haunting words that describe those of us who do not know our own passion or who have failed to bring our values to work:

"The Song I came to sing is left
unsung, I spent my life stringing and
unstringing my instrument."

Some Ways to Get Started on the Path of Self

1. Create opportunities for people to identify their own values and how these can be put into action at work. Ask people to make the connection with the corporate vision/mission/goals and their values.

2. Build corporate values from the bottom up.
3. Persuade people to identify what sparks commitment and energy at work.
4. Coach someone to help him or her find his or her passion. Ask the person questions that clarify what he or she wants out of work and how more of that could be brought into his or her current job.
5. Build a career development program that allows people to ask, "What could I do in the company that is closer to my passion?"

Exercise: Assessing Progress on the Path of Self

The following questions allow for an initial assessment of the progress you and your organization have already made on this path. The assessment is meant to guide your exploration, as opposed to provide definitive quantitative assessment of the state of your Corporate Soul.

1 = strongly agree
2 = agree
3 = disagree
4 = strongly disagree

___ The job I am in presently feels like "my passion."
___ I am true to myself in my present job situation/company.
___ The present work that I am involved in is important to me personally.
___ The job I am in now is mostly just a "job."
___ The role I play in my present career fits me.
___ Our company has a method in place for staff members to assess their careers, development goals, and desires.
___ Our company helps people identify their personal values and then discover ways that they align with the values of the company
___ In our company people are encouraged to "be themselves" in terms of how they behave, dress, and act.

___ Discussions about passion, commitment, and personal values are a common occurrence in our company.

Reflection

Based on the previous answers, what are the areas of potential growth for you? What about your company? In the areas of greatest opportunity, identify an example or two that exemplifies how you know growth is needed?

_____

_____

_____

_____

_____

Group Reflection & Action

If your whole leadership team is reading the book, use the previous mini-assessment and work as a group on the following exercises.

Individual Reflection & Action

Take the time now to reflect on what you have read about this path. Using the assessment above, what are some actions you could take right away to begin to tread more fully the Path of Self in your work? Identify just one or two actions to get you started as opposed to a large number that will not be implemented. Use "the ways to get started" as a guide.

_____

_____

_____

_____

_____

_____

Exercise: Unmasking Yourself at Work

Ask yourself the question, "Who am I at work?"
Write down words that describe you at work. Mark
those that are most authentic (reveal your soul) and
those that are most mask-like (conceal your soul).

_____

_____

_____

_____

_____

_____

_____

_____

_____

_____

Exercise: Bringing More of Yourself to Work

Reflect on the ways in which your present work is a
"Rubleman suit" and the ways in which you mask
your soul behind a persona at work. Then identify
the parts of yourself you wish to bring more into
your work.

_____

_____

_____

_____

_____

_____

_____

_____

"You ask me for a motto. Here it is: Service."
—ALBERT SCHWEITZER

"Do your work with the welfare of others always in your mind. By devotion to selfless work one attains the supreme goal of life."
—BHAGAVAD GITA

5

The Path of Contribution: Why Making a Difference Makes All the Difference

All wisdom traditions remind us that working with a sense of contribution and of service is essential to the soul's well-being. In the Tibetan Buddhist tradition it is stated, "You have this precious human body in order to serve other living beings." The soul awakens when our work is directed toward contributing to something larger than immediate personal needs. Yet few individuals and even fewer companies tap the energy that can be released by the power of contribution. The second path, the Path of Contribution, is about discovering the ways in which our work serves a larger purpose and about leaders who can help people see the deeper meaning of corporate endeavors.

Good Tired or Bad Tired

John learned about the power of contribution from his grandfather, a shipyard worker. A Canadian immigrant who left Nova Scotia during the Great Depression, John's grandfather had come to New England in search of work. For almost three decades he worked long days repairing ships in dry dock. He took pride in serving his adopted country by sending ships back to sea with a new lease on life and was known by his coworkers as a man who served others with kindness and compassion. He came home most nights very tired. "But it is a good tired," he would say. "A good tired is when you have spent everything you have and you know in your heart you accomplished something! A bad tired is when you have spent all you have, but it meant nothing to anyone."

What kind of tired have you produced at the end of a work day? Is it a good tired that renews commitment and awakens passion? Do people in your organization go home at the end of the week with a bad or a good tired? Do they know their efforts have an aim that goes beyond their own or even the shareholders' personal desires? Many workers lack the sense that the work they do makes any difference or that their efforts contribute anything of real value.

Beyond Surviving

Many leaders have asked us, "Why don't people work harder for us? Don't they know their jobs are on the line?" What these leaders fail to see is that few people give 150 percent because their job is on the line. It is sheer fantasy to believe people will sustain their best level only to survive. Indeed, the tougher times get, the more organizations need to call on a motivation that runs deeper than just the need to survive. Survival is a way of just hanging on while hoping for a better day. Tapping a deeper motivation based on a sense of real contribution draws on a source of sustainable commitment.

The soul desires a purpose that goes beyond just keeping a job or surviving the next organizational shakeup. The ultimate irony for organizations and their leaders is that it is those with the most talent and ambition—and therefore the most to contribute to the corporate enterprise—who may have the greatest need to see the definable difference their work makes. They are like the canaries in a mine. Their souls are sensitive to the toxic fumes of purposeless work. When work becomes devoid of meaning, their commitment and focus begin to weaken and they leave.

The Soul Wants to Make a Difference

When we ask people about their 150-percent experiences—those times when their work is most fulfilling, when they are most committed and alive—they speak of when their efforts make a difference to someone, of knowing their product brought lasting value and benefit to others. Recognizing the value of their efforts releases a current of enthusiasm. Consciously developing such an awareness of service and making a difference is what we call the Path of Contribution.

The Path of Contribution answers the questions, "Why are we doing this? What difference does my work make?" The Path of Contribution taps the innate motivation of the soul to use one's inner talents in service of a worthy goal.

Accumulation Versus Contribution

The gospel of Matthew speaks directly to the Path of Contribution. Jesus said, "He who seeks to save himself, will lose himself. But he who loses himself for my sake, he will find himself." Jesus knew an essential truth of the human soul: Its energy comes more from legacy and community than from having enough to pay the mortgage. When we see work as a means to an end (that is, pay, power, retirement) we miss its more essential and profound value. In terms of Corporate Soul, this passage contrasts two approaches to work. One focuses on self-centered, isolated desires—the small self. The other focuses on "losing" this small self and instead focusing on a larger, wiser, soul-enlivening vision, as Jesus himself models.

This teaching points to a paradox most modern people and organizations do not fully understand. When our work energies focus on saving the small self, that collection of wholly personal desires and goals, then our connection to the soul withers. When our work energies are consciously directed toward a larger purpose, however, we find ourselves enlivened by a sense of soulful fulfillment.

Having personal desires is, in and of itself, not the problem. These are part of our human nature. And it is not that the objects of desire—the VCRs, sports equipment, vacations, and such—are necessarily bad. The wisdom traditions simply want us to see these objects for what they are—VCRs, sports equipment, vacations—and to understand the path to fulfillment, purpose, and meaning lies in another direction. No matter how hard we run in the direction of our desires, the traditions tell us, the soul-satisfying sense of making a valuable contribution will elude us.

The wisdom traditions are not asking us to choose between a new television set and a new state of consciousness. Appliances, sofas, and cars all have their place in a balanced life. The wisdom traditions certainly are asking us to understand that when the corporate crisis is one of commitment and passion, the solution lies in tapping what Gandhi called the "soul force." Directing our work primarily down the road of accumulation rather than the Path of Contribution leads us on a detour away from Corporate Soul.

Feeding Hungry Ghosts

In the East, a soul that is constantly seeking its own reward and forever trying to feed its own desires is called a hungry ghost. A hungry ghost is a soul in a perpetual state of hunger, endlessly consuming things but never feeling satisfied. Our culture tends to reinforce the hungry ghost mindset, promising the feeling of personal fulfillment via consumerism. This mindset is carried into the workplace as an attitude of entitlement instead of service. When a company depends on "outside" rewards to motivate performance, it creates a work place full of hungry ghosts. The hungry ghosts ask incessantly, "What are you doing for me? What can I get from you?" When all our efforts focus on our own small self desires, we lose the very sense of soul fulfillment we are supposedly seeking.

Trapped in the cycle of the hungry ghost, we become like the man in the Sufi story who, after paying a bargain price for a basket of hot chili peppers, started to eat them. The more he ate the more his mouth burned. Soon tears streamed down his cheeks. When a friend asked why he kept eating the burning peppers. The man replied, "I keep waiting for a sweet one!"

Only when we get outside the small self and invest our energies in a larger purpose do we reestablish a living connection to the soul. Recognizing that our work is of genuine service to others, we can draw from the soulful well of commitment throughout the work day.

Making the Inside Connection

Not long ago a chartered bus filled with passengers passed us on the freeway. Above the front window, where the sign should have indicated a destination, was written "The Wrong Bus." Many companies have been riding the wrong bus for years trying to call forth deeper commitment from workers.

Most organizations strive to increase commitment by offering people something for themselves—more money, better benefits, a corner office, a more impressive title, workout centers, improved food facilities, time off, and so on. Many of us try to reignite our own commitment similarly, with goals of advancement and financial gain. All of these have their appropriate function but, ironically, most can only be enjoyed when one is not at work!

The Path of Contribution looks to the work itself as the source of meaning and fulfillment. This Path focuses not on perks and symbols but on strengthening the conscious connection between everyday efforts and their contribution to a higher purpose. Commitment arises naturally when we know our work amounts to something beyond ourselves when we know the energies we expend are converted into something of value to others. Finding this inner key to motivation means looking deeply into our work and discovering its hidden higher purpose. How to look deeply is illustrated in the following tale.

Finding the Key

Mulla Nasruddin was outside on his hands and knees below a lantern when a friend approached.

"What are you doing, Mulla?" the friend asked.

"I am looking for my key. I've lost it."

His friend got down on his hands and knees. They both searched for a long time in the dirt. Finding nothing, his friend finally asked, "Where exactly did you lose the key?"

Nasruddin replied, "I lost it in the house."

"Then why are we looking out here?" the friend demanded.

The Mulla answered, "There is much more light out here."

Like the Mulla, most organizations prefer to search for the key to commitment in the light of the familiar. It is easier, after all, to stick with known strategies—reward systems, bonuses, incentives, and perks. We are familiar with these things; we know how to report and measure them. These kinds of programs are needed, but they are not enough to unleash the power of the soul. We must leave the known for the unknown and investigate the inner source of lasting commitment for that to happen.

This starts with uncovering the valuable, though potentially hidden, purpose of our work; it means recognizing the purpose our organization fulfills that goes beyond the bottom line; and it means articulating to others how their efforts contribute to a larger purpose.

The Opportunity Is Always Present

How do we make the shift from the hungry ghost's obsession with the small self to the awakened soul's sense of purpose, realization, and service? We begin by cultivating an awareness of the opportunities for contribution and service that are already present in our work.

When Moses encountered the burning bush, he was told, "Take off your shoes, you are standing on holy ground." It seems strange. How could Moses not recognize the spiritual opportunity before him? But there he was standing in front of something absolutely holy and he did not act accordingly. This teaching shows us how easy it can be to stand in the presence of something sacred and still overlook it.

In the workplace this is particularly true as we have been trained to believe the spiritual, the sacred, and the soul have no place on the job. This assumption blinds us to existing opportunities for soulful contribution and fulfillment. There are already hundreds of possibilities for service and contribution in our present conditions. In unawareness, we often walk right by them. Like Moses, we are already on holy ground. To someone who is in a hurry even a burning bush can be overlooked as another shrub and simply treated as an ordinary part of the landscape.-The Path of Contribution starts with the rediscovery that our present work and current interactions are where we can immediately make a difference.

Don't Wait to Save the World

Sometimes, it takes a strong reminder to call our attention to everyday opportunities to serve. The burning bush can come in unexpected forms. When John entered graduate school it was the middle of a school year. Studying for the ministry at the time, he was eager to find a part-time job to "save the world." Unfortunately, since it was the middle of the term, all the part-time jobs to save the world were already taken. The only job he could find was as a postal clerk at a drug store in a poor neighborhood on the south side of Chicago.

Over a period of weeks, John began to hate the job. Spending twenty-five hours behind a counter when he could be out saving the world was torturous. In time, he even began to hate the customers and their requests. Many customers came to the counter for money orders to pay their bills, sometimes requesting up to ten at a time. Writing money orders was a tedious and time-consuming task. Frustration combined with his middle-class background would have John looking at the line of people and thinking to himself, "For goodness' sake, get a checking account!"

Summer approached, and John had resigned himself to long, hot summer months of writing money orders and selling stamps when a letter offering an internship at a cancer ward came through.

Armed with a new-found "Who cares! I'm out of here" attitude, John arrived at the postal station the next rainy Chicago morning. The usual line of customers was waiting. The third customer in line was an elderly black woman in a trench coat whose small brown hat was dripping raindrops onto her shoulders. She asked for four money orders. Just to be friendly and cheered by his short-timer attitude, John asked her how she was. "Not well," the woman sighed, "my daughter is over in the hospital and they say she is going to die in the next two days. I should be there with her. But if I don't pay my rent today they will evict me."

Their conversation continued for a few more moments and John offered a few words of encouragement. As she left, this old woman walked about eight feet away, then turned back to the counter, interrupting the next customer. She grabbed John's forearm gently and looked into his eyes. She whispered, "Sonny, I just wanted to say thank you for making an otherwise dismal day bearable. You are so kind."

As she walked away John thought of the months he spent behind that counter wasting his time inwardly complaining and cussing the customers. He wondered how many opportunities for service and soul connection had been missed while he waited for a "save the world" job. In that moment, John saw the purpose and contribution his routine work provided his customers. Whether one is a clerk in a store, a worker in a factory, or a manager in a company, the opportunities to serve are endless if we have but the eyes to see them.

Uncovering Holy Ground

There are many for whom the vision of contribution and service has dimmed. Leaders who wish to issue the wake-up call, "Remove your shoes! You are on holy ground!" would be wise to begin with themselves and discover their own everyday opportunities for contribution and service. From that basis it is easier to move into the organization to support others in cultivating an awareness of their own holy ground.

Discovering Contribution

The Buddha said, "Mind is the forerunner of all actions." A shift of mind naturally evolves into a shift of behavior and ultimately into new results. The organizer of a professional association meeting told us that her previous job was one that she had come to hate. She disliked the company and the product and saw little personal reward for her efforts. Besides, she felt the job was not a good fit for her skills and interests. Like many, Joanne fell into a pattern of constant complaining about her job. "One day I realized I was spending most of my energy looking for things to complain about," she told us. "So I decided to do a mental one-eighty." Joanne decided to make a list of blessings she experienced at work. She reflected on the things she was grateful for in her job and how she felt she was contributing. The list was very short: "I get a paycheck and the weekend starts every Friday at five o'clock."

Over the next few weeks Joanne kept working with the list. At the end of each day she would reflect on the blessings she experienced. Soon she found herself trying to create experiences to go on the list. She began to look for opportunities to create blessings instead of waiting for them to come to her. By the time she left the job one year later, for a position better suited to her interests, Joanne had a notebook full of blessings. She concluded, "It is amazing what happens when you start to look for blessings. Now I create opportunities every day to make a difference and to be grateful."

Joanne's practice is a soulful discipline. It is a method for calling attention to what is truly rewarding. It is a way to put the mind of the hungry ghost to rest and to nourish the soul with acts of service.

Leaders cannot awaken the Corporate Soul until they are awake to the deeper possibilities of their own work. We can begin to inspire others after our daily efforts become a clear expression of service and contribution. In this way a most personal task becomes a first step to corporate renewal.

Help People See Their Contribution

One way of helping people see the contribution of their work is to get them closer to the customers or people whom they serve. In any job it is easy to forget the impact we have on customers because so often they don't tell us. When our colleague David was a manager in a hospital, he would occasionally come out of a business meeting and see a patient on a gurney in a hallway and surprise himself by thinking, "Oh my, there are sick people in this place." Of course he knew this, but the nature of his work as a manager tended to insulate him from the fundamental purpose, indeed the primary contribution of the hospital: caring for the ill.

It is easy in any job to get so caught up in completing our list of tasks we forget the end result toward which these tasks are aimed. When our vision narrows down to the task at hand, the larger purpose of our endeavors can grow dim. Leading others on the Path of Contribution means helping people make the connection between their to-do lists and the contribution their efforts make to others.

Better than telling people that what they do matters is letting them hear it from the customers directly. We work with several organizations that videotaped focus groups of customers and presented an edited version to all staff. Listening to these frank discussions by customers of what service means to them along with specific incidents of good and bad service has had a powerful impact on employee commitment and motivation. Manipulative efforts to improve service behavior pale in comparison to the simple act of being reminded by the people we serve that what we do matters.

The Higher Purpose of Work

Many companies spend millions of dollars on ad campaigns to convince customers they care about their needs. Yet how many spend anywhere near that amount of attention or budget on helping people who deliver service see that what they do has a higher purpose?

Along with listening to customers, the Path of Contribution unfolds by identifying how our work is in fact a contribution. We use an exercise to help shift people's thinking from the to-do list to their purpose by asking a two-part question. First we ask, "What is the business purpose of your work?" Most people will respond with statements such as, "To build great products so that the company makes a profit," or "To help our customers solve their accounting problems." Then we ask, "What is the higher purpose of your work?" This question always starts an interesting conversation. Some people object to the implication there may even be a higher (or deeper) purpose to something they had always thought of as just a job. Most, however, are intrigued. Their soul senses something.

Answers to the higher-purpose questions have included, "To help people and society prosper," "To open up children's minds and creativity so they love to learn," or "To prolong life through scientific breakthroughs." Many have become so accustomed to seeing their work solely in economic terms, the higher purpose to which they are contributing can seem at first like a fantasy. It is not. By including awareness of the top line—the higher purpose with the bottom line—the financial performance we gain a fuller understanding of what our work is all about. The Corporate Soul embraces both the top and the bottom lines.

Sometimes we stumble onto the meaning of our contribution. A manager at a medical device company went to visit his father-in-law in the hospital. The older man lay in bed hooked up to a ventilator made by the manager's company. "Standing in the room, I realized what our company was all about," he told us. "Seeing my father-in-law being kept alive by our product made me feel grateful to all my coworkers. I saw that what we do really matters."

Recently we came across a simple way of helping people uncover the deeper meaning of their work. In the midst of a traditional team-building session, we made a slight change in questioning. Instead of asking what the senior team wanted to accomplish for the company, we asked, "What do you want to be your legacy to your community? To your organization? To your customers? To your staff? Exchanging the word "outcome" with the word "legacy" promoted a different kind of thinking. Group members said things such as, "Creating jobs for people in our small town," "Allowing families to keep the next generation here," "Working at a place that nourishes the soul," and so on.

Thinking about the outcomes we want is very different from focusing on the legacy we want to leave behind. The very language we use can obscure or illuminate the deeper significance of our efforts. Why not try it in your place of work, beginning with yourself: What would you like the legacy of your leadership team to be? Beyond visions of best and greatest, what is the higher purpose and lasting impact of your work? It is often the apprehension of the deeper purpose that puts zeal into the everyday tasks that must be accomplished for a business to remain competitive.

Contribution Is Where You Find It

Unlike the manager of the ventilator, most of our work does not deal with life or death activities. Fortunately, the soul does not demand such high stakes to ignite a sense of meaning. The soul does not require a chance to save the world to find purpose and fulfillment. Rather the soul awakens in response to serving, no matter how "small" the effort. Mother Teresa has said, "There are no great acts. There are only small acts, done with great love."

The Path of Contribution links our small daily acts to that greater love or service in which we participate. For the data processing manager at a large university this means seeing that his work keeps students records orderly and helps them achieve their goals in life. For a senior executive of an international hotel chain it means reminding his managers they are not just creating profits for the company or a feather in the hat of their own advancement. As leaders they are there to serve the people who serve their guests.

People Not Paper

In following the Path of Contribution, one firm instituted a "People Not Paper" campaign to shift the way service representatives viewed the telephone-based relationships they had with customers. Never seeing a customer face-to-face can create a sense of being unconnected and lead to impersonal, mechanical interactions. The president told us, "We wanted to underline that every call we receive is, in fact, a call from a person.Unless we can meet that customer as a person, in a professional and understanding way, we will not be able to solve their technical or human problem. And in our business, these two problems always come together."

Monthly meetings with customers were established and real people who had once just been voices over the telephone came in to talk about what it meant to be on the other end of the phone. One employee remarked, "It is helpful to hear from the customer directly about what works and what doesn't. What I do everyday affects their lives. Seeing them in person has changed how I think about our business."

Organizations on the Path of Contribution need to find ways to amplify the voice of the customer so people throughout the organization can listen. How is the voice of the customer heard in your company? How do people learn of the difference their product or service makes to others? How do people hear from their customers, "This is the difference your work makes for me!"?

Serving Beyond the Corporate Walls

The first scene in the movie *City Slickers* depicts the Billy Crystal character talking to his son's second grade class about what he does at work. He is an account executive at a radio station. His attempt at explaining his job to a group of eight-year-olds becomes an agonizing exercise in self-revelation. "I sell time. I sell air time," he mumbles to the stone-faced class. In their blank expressions he sees the purposelessness of what he does. "I sell air," he concludes with a grimace. We know that inside his soul is crying.

Clearly, not all work has the same intrinsic value or potential for service and contribution. Some of us may conclude like the character in *City Slickers* we "sell air." In this sense, some companies have an advantage over others in pursuing the Path of Contribution. There are even situations when the soul recognizes that one's work contributes in destructive ways to the community or the global environment. What can leaders do in companies where the product or service does not seem to make a contribution? How does such a company find ways to appeal to the deeper commitment the soul requires?

First, it is critical to understand all workplaces offer the potential for service in the moments of communication between people. Whatever we do—whether saving lives as a firefighter or delivering pizzas—there are moments of human meeting that have the potential to manifest grace and compassion. As John experienced in that postal substation in inner-city Chicago, if our eyes are focused on service, there are opportunities in the most unlikely situations.

When an organization's production activity has a negative impact on society or the environment, however, we may have to go beyond the scope of normal business to create an authentic sense of contribution and meaning. An example of this is a utility company in New England that involved workers in a decision to plant a million trees in Latin America as a way of compensating for the pollutants their plants emit into the atmosphere. Recognizing that energy is important to society, they also realized their industrial process harms the environment. This tree-planting project was a way of following the Path of Contribution that went beyond the work itself. Some leading organizations give sabbaticals for executives to work on social service and community development causes. Other organizations involve staff in working with organizations such as Habitat for Humanity, which builds affordable housing in disadvantaged neighborhoods.

The link from such activities to the bottom line is not direct. No accounting methodology values how such efforts contribute to commitment, motivation, creativity, or performance. In that sense, enlightened leaders who extend the Path of Contribution beyond the walls of the organization are taking a leap of faith.

Each of us knows personally, however, that as the soul awakens it suffuses our actions with energy and power. Perhaps we need only ask ourselves what we felt like the last time we really believed we were contributing.

The Soul Rejects Fear

John's grandfather taught him to distinguish between good tired and bad tired. Many people in our organizations today know the effects of bad tired. They have worked long and hard only to wonder whether the time, energy, and effort they have given has produced anything of lasting value. In a climate of doing more with less it is all too easy for leaders to emphasize "our jobs are at stake" as a reason for increased commitment. But fear tactics, no matter how "realistic," do not inspire the soul. Leaders are called to find a way of fusing the realistic challenges of the marketplace with the higher purpose of the workplace in their message to people. Overstressing the "realistic" challenges leads to indifference and burnout. Commitment and passion can be unleashed at work, but the primary stimulant for unleashing them is to unite business purposes and higher purposes into a single message.

A regional health authority in Canada faced a situation of decreasing revenues, changing expectations, and growing demand. Speaking to the 18,000 staff members, the leader of the company underlined their obligation to a future where rising health care needs would run head long into a decreasing tax base.

"In this environment," he said, "efforts at efficiency are not just about saving money but also about finding ways to provide quality medicine today without bankrupting the next generation."

His message anchored the tremendous challenges of the moment in a broader vision that included serving the next generation.

Leaders who really value the deeper meaning of work go beyond speech-making and build organizational structures that support the higher purpose. They make tangible changes in job requirements, policies, and procedures to promote service and contribution. No amount of snake oil will unlock the soul's commitment. The soul wants something worthy to engage in, something valuable to serve, something meaningful to commit to. Finding these the soul is willing to expend great effort and experience the good tired that comes from walking the Path of Contribution.

Some Ways to Get Started on the Path of Contribution

1. Find a way to get closer to customers—go out and talk to them, videotape them, telephone them. Remind yourself and others of the difference your work makes.
2. Find a way to "amplify" the voice of the customer in your company so people can actually hear the difference they are making
3. Create a clear, simple message that unites business realities with the higher purpose. Make this your "battle cry." Repeat the message consistently.
4. Begin a list of things you are grateful for in your work—ways you feel you have contributed—then look at the pattern and create more of those things.
5. Identify a "customer" situation common in your area of responsibility where staff might miss the

real needs and opportunity to serve this customer. Share your insights or coach staff to see the impact.

6. Create forums at staff meetings where people can share when they made a difference in the last week. Make this a fun and genuine time of connection.
7. Find a "community" cause to which your company can contribute. Be sure it allows for a "hands-on" opportunity for people to participate.
8. Identify the deeper meaning of your work. What does it contribute to others? Who do you serve?
9. Identify the legacy you want to leave behind.

Exercise: Finding the Holy Ground

The Path of Contribution begins by serving the people who already surround us. Who will you meet today? Customers? Coworkers? Bosses? What can you do or say that would be of service?

_____

_____

_____

_____

_____

_____

_____

_____

Exercise: Assessing Progress on the Path of Contribution

The statements below allow for an initial assessment of the progress you and your organization have already made on this path. The assessment is meant to guide your exploration, as opposed to provide some definitive quantitative assessment of the state of your Corporate Soul. For each statement, answer as to how true this is of you in your present work situation and then for your company.

1 = strongly agree
2 = agree
3 = disagree
4 = strongly disagree

___ The customer's voice is amplified in our company so people hear from their customers the difference they make.

___ Our company has significant ways of giving back to the community that directly involve our people in a hands-on manner.

___ As a leader, I remind people regularly of the difference our work makes.

___ Our company has feedback loops in place to help people see the outcome of their work.

___ I am aware of the significant ways my job makes a contribution to a worthy purpose.

___ I am aware of daily moments of holy ground/ meeting in which I can make a difference to others.

___ Our company regularly celebrates when individuals or teams have completed a significant project or goal.

___ In our company we have helped people recognize the contribution our products and services make to others.

___ Discussions about contribution, service, and the difference our work makes are a common occurrence around our company.

Reflection

Based on the previous responses, what are the areas of potential growth for you?

_____

_____

_____

_____

Your company?

_____

_____

_____

_____

What actions will you take to deepen your sense of purpose?

_____

_____

_____

_____

What actions will you take to help others deepen their sense of purpose?

_____

_____

_____

_____

"My miraculous power and spiritual activity:
Drawing water and chopping wood."
—LAYMAN P'ANG

"Perform every act sacramentally." —BHAGAVAD GITA

6

The Path of Craft: Details That Make the Difference

A practical measure of our soulfulness at work is the degree to which we are present, aware, and participating moment-by-moment in the work at hand. Only by engagement in the present moment can there be movement in the soul's journey. If our body is the only part of us present in a meeting and 75 percent of us is waiting impatiently in the parking lot, there is little hope of awakening Corporate Soul. As long as we are sitting at our desks daydreaming of other times and places we cannot release the soul's energy in our work. When people bring only a fraction of their potential into the workplace, there is little hope an organization will stay competitive in the current marketplace. The Path of Craft is about creating ways that people can be more engaged in the daily moments of their work and thus produce stellar results.

You Must Be Present

When a local elementary school sponsored a raffle to raise funds for new programs, "Need Not Be Present to Win" was stamped on the back of each ticket. The same cannot be said for awakening Corporate Soul. Our presence is absolutely required. If we are not present, the soul is absent.

In this regard work is the same as meditation. The Zen tradition states there are only two activities that take place at a monastery: sitting and sweeping. Sitting is the practice of silent meditation, which requires a commitment of total presence and absolute focus. Sweeping, meaning all the tasks of maintaining the buildings and grounds, equally requires a commitment of total presence and absolute focus. Both sitting and sweeping offer the mindful practitioner a doorway to soulful awakening.

Our interviews with people regarding their experiences of soulfulness at work echoed this theme. An integral aspect of soulful work is, in the words of one engineer, "total immersion." People described experiences of timelessness as they became fully absorbed in the process of their work. Sandra, a member of the marketing department at a high-tech firm, spoke of "becoming so absorbed in my work everything else fades away." This practice of total immersion and one pointed focus is central to what we call the *Path of Craft.*

The End Is Not Near

Following the Path of Craft draws us into the process of working in the present moment. On the Path of Craft we develop intense enjoyment in the moment-to-moment action of our work, turning even the most mundane task into a soulful meditation. On the Path of Craft we don't just celebrate end results; we learn to enjoy the journey.

The wisdom of this path is in seeing that end results are, in fact, not the end at all. Everything is part of an ongoing process. Following the Path of Craft is all about relishing the journey, appreciating the process, and fully participating in the passing moments that form the living body of our work.

A perfect example of these principles in action is the Cathedral of Saint John the Divine, an imposing stone edifice that majestically overlooks New York City's Upper West Side. This magnificent structure, a living testament to the human spirit and the glories of craftsmanship, has been continuously worked on for over a hundred years, and the "end" is not in sight. Work is projected to continue for perhaps another seventy years. Craftsmen from many countries continue to shape and renew the building, carving in stone, working in glass, paint, and wood. Most will not be alive when the structure is "finished," if such a term is even appropriate. As craftsmen they work diligently and lovingly in the present moment bringing their attention, skill, and knowledge to the task at hand.

Redefining Completion

It is interesting to consider how workers can stay motivated when faced with a project that will not be finished in their lifetime. In a culture that worships results and where attention spans are measured in seconds, it is interesting to consider how workers could stay authentically interested in a two-hundred-year project that may not be completed in their lifetime.

This is one of the secrets of the Path of Craft. On this path motivation is realized by generating a profound sense of completion in the present moment. Completion, thus, does not mean that the job is over. Completion is redefined to mean *complete participation,* which always and only occurs in the present moment. When we are completely participating there is no room for doubt, confusion, fear, or expectation. In this state of total involvement we do not look forward nor backward. Where we are, in the present moment, is more than enough. This is how completion is defined on the Path of Craft. As Albert Camus wisely wrote, "Real generosity towards the future consists in giving all to what is present."

Certainly organizations and leaders clearly need to consider the future. Anticipating possibilities; imagining what may occur; anticipating as yet undefined changes; inventing possibilities—all these modes of future focused thought are essential to sustain a thriving enterprise. The Path of Craft introduces an often neglected way of thinking and acting that complements future focus. By always fixating on the finish line, the destination, the end result, we miss out on the process of getting there. Acknowledging the process, celebrating small steps, and appreciating daily efforts are ways that leaders can begin to cultivate a sense of craft and value the moment-to-moment aspect of work.

Soul awakens in the daily moments of work—in meetings, in telephone calls, in customer interactions, in tasks—and if these moments are not alive with energy, the final outcome will also be lifeless. As one friend put it, "The challenge is to actually be present when our work happens." If the moment-to-moment work we do lacks soul energy, so the end result of our work will lack vitality. Many people are just searching for meaning in their work; they are also seeking the experience of meaningful presence.

Attention to Detail

One of the soul-crushing results of the industrial revolution has been the development of "industry without art," according to Ananda Coomarswamy. The Path of Craft involves a revival of the soul's creative and artistic powers in every aspect of the workplace and focuses on the process of transforming raw materials into works of utility and beauty. Craft is never art for art's sake as it always serves a useful end. But without a sense of artistry, beauty, and creativity in our work the soul will not come alive.

The soul awakens in the presence of mindfulness and artistic integrity no matter where it is found. One of the ways this manifests at work is in attention to detail. Go into a workplace and watch how much or little attention is paid to details and you will experience a soul "barometer." We experienced this attending a banquet at a Marriott Hotel. When we entered the large ballroom filled with more than a hundred tables, a server stood by each table at total attention with a napkin draped over one arm. When all guests were seated, in a synchronized motion the staff bowed to the assembled throng. Their faces beamed as they executed their choreography, and the guests responded with spontaneous applause.

In our hometown of San Diego at the self-proclaimed "World Famous Hand Car Wash," workers turn each wash into a symphony of craft. These are mostly new immigrants paid little to do a task few line up to do. Yet with no supervisors in evidence, the humor, enthusiasm, and attention to detail the workers bring to their work turns this "nonartistic" task into a demonstration of artistry.

On Southwest Airlines, bubbly attendants compete for who can come up with the funniest version of the safety instruction ritual. Everyone enjoys it, and people actually listen to what could be lifesaving information. On other major airlines, this task is totally routine. When it is not performed by a video monitor, it is slowly droned out by workers who miss the potential artistry that could be brought to this basic part of their job.

How do we begin to infuse the daily tasks of our work with this necessary soul vitality? A starting place is to rediscover the craft of our work, which starts by paying greater attention to details. By following the Path of Craft we can learn to devote full attention to the details of our work and lovingly pursue artistic excellence in seemingly nonartistic tasks. This approach is described by the contemporary meditation master Thich Nhat

Hahn who said, "Each act must be carried out in mindfulness. Each act is a rite, a ceremony."

Craft may seem like an archaic word unsuited to the challenges facing modern corporations. But we have seen how by restoring the notion of craft to work people raise their level of performance and enthusiasm. The soul appreciates reincorporating a sense of aesthetics and harmony into the workplace. Turning every action into an act of beauty, which may seem out of place in a world focused on expedience and efficiency, is fundamental to the Path of Craft. As Gandhi said, "There is more to life than increasing its speed."

The Path of Craft brings up some basic questions: How is our organization helping people bring artistry to their work? What is being done to reinforce the power of attending to details?

Working With Raw Materials

Every work process involves the transformation of raw materials into works of utility and beauty. The "raw materials" of one job may be as tangible as sheet metal while in another the raw materials may be as abstract as numbers or words. We all work with some set of raw materials, regardless of their relative solidity. And in pursuing the Path of Craft it is necessary to determine the raw materials with which we work.

In our case, as speakers, the raw materials we use are ideas, voice tones and rhythms, words, and body gestures we use when communicating with our audiences. The craft of speaking involves fusing these raw materials into a useful and moving presentation.

Having determined one's raw materials, the next step on the Path of Craft is to identify what it would mean to combine these elements in an ultimately useful and beautiful manner. What would your work look like if it were to combine the highest expressions of utility and beauty? What would it mean to be the Picasso or Mozart in your field? Martin Luther King, Jr., said, "If you are called to be a street sweeper, you should sweep streets as Michelangelo painted, or Beethoven composed music, or Shakespeare wrote poetry."

By requiring us to think in terms of superlatives and to envision our work as beautiful, the Path of Craft asks us to elevate our standards of performance and strive for artistry in even the most mundane work process. We love the statement by Abraham Maslow, a pioneer in the field of human development, who said, "A first-rate soup is more creative than a second-rate painting." Even if our work is not the sort shown in museums or recorded on compact discs, it is our craft and it is the place where our creativity can shine.

Release Creative Forces

The soul is by nature creative. This creativity can be called forth by clearly defined standards of craftsmanship—standards that include a sense of utility and beauty. The soul wants to come forth, to express itself and manifest its inner richness. Our experience in helping companies improve in the area of customer service illustrates how the Corporate Soul awakens when people are engaged in establishing high standards of craftsmanship for themselves.

Customer service turnarounds begin by creating a steering group of top-performing staff members from all levels of the company weighted toward the front line. This group of people are already on the Path of Craft, they are the organization's master craftsmen and women. As such they are given the mandate of upgrading the customer service standards throughout the organization. We help them do this via a three-step process:

Step 1: The group interviews customers to identify what great service means to them as customers.

Step 2: Then the group defines new standards for customer service based on customers' input and their own sense of what makes for great service.

Step 3: The group communicates these new standards, in partnership with management, to the entire organization.

In all of the organizations we have worked with, two interesting things occurred as a result of this process. First, service improved as staff members persuade their peers that a new level of performance is both needed and attractive. Second, a sense of enthusiasm and commitment emerged in the companies, many of which had been bureaucracies wherein the soul's heartbeat had long ago slowed to being almost undetectable.

In many wisdom traditions the soul is compared to a well. Those of us who have gone camping know that to get water out of a well, we need to put a small amount of priming water in. Having primed the pump, the abundant resources of the well are released. High standards of craftsmanship, that people themselves participate in creating, are the Corporate Soul's priming water. By pouring these standards in we can then move into action, start pumping, and watch as the creativity, enthusiasm, and energy of the Corporate Soul pours forth.

Craft Is Timeless

In our most focused moments on the Path of Craft time is suspended. This is illustrated by an experience that Dan, an extraordinary designer of computer chips, told us about. He had been working intensely for many days on a new product and gradually found himself moving "so deeply into the design I was no longer in everyday time. I just dropped off the clock and went to a place of pure thought. New ideas and solutions seemed to flow into my mind effortlessly." Dan had found what the poet t. s. eliot called "the still point in the turning world."

All wisdom traditions speak of this motionless center. It is the place where transformation and creativity occur. Breakthroughs in technology design, market strategy, work processes, and interpersonal dynamics all arise from this place, which is in the center of the soul. When one is situated in this still point, time as it is measured normally ceases to exist. Many athletes have described their experiences of touching into this timeless zone and discovering a virtually bottomless reservoir of energy. Mystics have described it as a place of illumination and wholeness. Although it is less frequently written about, such moments occur also in the context of work. The Path of Craft cultivates our familiarity with this still point by encouraging us to practice mindful absorption in the work at hand. The focused attention of the craftsman is akin to the centered mind of the Zen or yoga master. For when we become mindfully absorbed in our work we are practicing a form of meditation in action.

Effects of Scattered Minds

Imagine an organization filled with workers whose minds are scattered, distracted, and disengaged. Then imagine the opposite, a workplace where people are focused, fully participating, and mindful. The differences in terms of the quality of the work and the quality of commitment are obvious.

The wisdom traditions are emphatic regarding the negative effects of a scattered mind on work and self. The scattering of the mind breaks our ability to connect with any sense of completeness or to engage effectively in the present moment. The scattered mind is easily distracted, cannot solve problems, and is habitually lost in the past or worrying about the future. Such a mind is a breeding ground for performance and interpersonal problems.

The wisdom traditions suggest the first step in overcoming the negative tendencies of the scattered mind is to recognize the difference between the experience of mindful focus and a scattered mind. The next step is to make efforts and take actions that encourage mindful presence, particularly in situations where it will be most challenging.

Be Here Now

When the semiconductor division of an international communications firm was going through a major organizational renewal, people spent a lot of time in group meetings. Recognizing the tendency for meetings to become "strange encounters of the absent minds" where people sit and talk but no activity of value is taking place, the entire organization adopted the slogan "Be Here Now." Placards with the slogan were posted in major meeting rooms. Presentations began with a slide printed with the slogan to remind people to be fully present physically, mentally, and spiritually so the organizational transformation would be successful. As anyone who has sat through many meetings knows, the ability to "Be Here Now" is no simple feat.

It is one of the leader's tasks on the Path of Craft to maintain a reasonable degree of mindful balance. We like to joke that leadership means being at least 51 percent present. This may sound like a low number but any careful observation of the workplace will reveal most people are functioning well below the 50 percent mark in terms of mindful presence. Of course, as the Corporate Soul really begins to awaken the requirements for leaders to continue their own development increases. Leaders who are not soulfully present cannot effectively help others shift from the scattered to the awakened mind.

Love of the Hands

We heard management authority Ken Blanchard echo the wisdom traditions when he said, "When you are working at your passion, you lose track of time." Organizations that support people in finding their true work, their passion, are skillfully encouraging the development of focused and engaged work.

On the Path of Craft we are looking for what we call the love of the hands. When we are engaged in such work our body relaxes and we tap into abundant energies. It is a physical response of being in synch. For one person this may happen when working with numbers. Working with numbers is the love of her hands. For another this could be through the conversations he has with customers. He loves to talk about his product, solve customer problems, and close deals. Selling is the love of his hands.

When we find the love of our hands we have found the work process that brings our soul alive. Interestingly, as the soul awakens we experience both more energy and more stillness. We have more energy to pour into our work for it is fed by love. We also have a sense of inner stillness, balance, and harmony. We aren't going against our own grain. The Buddhist Master Layman P'Ang writes, "My daily affairs are quite ordinary; but I am in total harmony with them. My miraculous power and spiritual activity: drawing water and carrying wood." Finding the love of our hands is like waking up to something we have always known. There is a part of us that already knows what we love to do. Doing that work brings our body and mind into the present moment. We awaken to the ordinary miracle of fulfilled work.

Death of a Soul

Many people are quite out of touch with the work that feeds their soul. They don't remember the love of their hands, and their body and soul suffer. In Arthur Miller's famous play *Death of a Salesman,* the antihero Willie Loman is a tragic figure, an ambitious salesman with limited potential who has been dead-ended and is finally let go by the company for which he works. Miller, writing in the 1950s, was ahead of his time in describing the corporation's propensity for spitting out middle-aged workers at a time when their souls are most vulnerable. Yet the real tragedy of the play is not revealed until the very last scene, which takes place after the funeral for Loman, who commits suicide. In that final scene, Willie's son Biff recognizes the essential tragedy of his father's life: He spent his entire life as a salesman but his real love was working with his hands. Willie loved working with his hands and in trying to be a salesman, he destroyed his soul and missed his life.

How can we tell if we are working at a craft that is not native to our soul? For many the inner mismatch will be felt as a persistent sense of being in the wrong place. For others it will be a sense of struggling uphill, constantly battling the odds and never gaining ground. For almost everyone there will be the inability to become joyfully immersed in the present moment. When we are not working at our true craft, we do not step, in the words of Rumi, "out of the circle of time and into the circle of love." Instead we watch the clock.

The search for the love of our hands can begin by recognizing those work activities during which time stops. What are the work processes that are innately attractive, compelling, and endlessly interesting? Following these clues leads us further on the Path of Craft.

Organizations & the Love of Hands

Leaders and managers can help people walk the Path of Craft by encouraging the practice of mindfulness. Leaders and organizations can also support people in discovering the love of their hands by giving candid feedback. If we see someone struggling down a career path that clearly does not fit their nature, talents, or soul, we have a responsibility to let this person know. In observing the performance of individuals, it is clear that some work awakens the soul and other work puts it to sleep. This is especially critical when someone is beginning a career and has not yet built up much momentum. Timely feedback can provide necessary redirection.

John had such an experience in his first career in ministry. He loved preaching and teaching but seemed ill suited to other parts of parish ministry. It was a kind, elderly woman who said to him following a Sunday morning sermon, "Son, you are quite a poor visitor. When you came to my house last week I thought you were going to fall asleep. But when you are up there on the pulpit, it is a thing of beauty. Speaking is your love." Her words rang true. This feedback, similar remarks from others, and his inner changes led John from the ministry to a new career as a speaker and organizational consultant.

Organizations also help people pursue the Path of Craft by taking time in the hiring process to determine not just whether someone can do a particular job but also where the person's passion lies. What would it mean to ask prospective employees to identify times when they have been at their best in their careers? By identifying times and places where their best was present, the applicants and interviewer can determine if the present job offers opportunities that will bring the soul alive.

Learning Is Not Boring

The Chinese word for boring consists of two characters: heart and killing. Boredom kills the heart. Sad but true. When work shrinks to the point that it cannot accommodate the soul, when tasks become so repetitive that there is no room for nuance or creativity then the heart and soul are killed by boredom.

The Path of Craft offers an antidote to this horrible state in the form of ongoing learning. Developing our artistry and excellence requires that we keep learning and developing our capabilities. The very word "craft" comes from the German meaning "power" and implies the bringing forth of our inner powers. To pursue craft means to perpetually bring forth our inner powers. And this means we must be forever learning.

Organizations that have embraced the philosophy of lifelong learning are already fulfilling this aspect of the Path of Craft. They are engaging workers in regular training in both technical and nontechnical skills, job rotation, and work redesign. In the most forward-thinking organizations, learning extends well beyond the parameters of the job description.

In our interviews with workers regarding Corporate Soul, one of the common themes was their desire for new challenges. People say their 150 percent comes out when they are stretched, when their work brings them into new areas of craft. For example, coal miners at a large power generation company sit on a task force that decides where to invest the company's pension fund. The miners have had to learn myriad new skills related to economic analysis, financial performance, and market prediction. For leaders whose vision does not include the Corporate Soul, it may seem irrelevant for these men to be engaged in such work, but an understanding of the Path of Craft dictates that such activities have innumerable benefits. The miners themselves speak of their deeper sense of responsibility and ownership, which shapes everything they do on the job.

In another case, a housekeeper's job in a hospital is redesigned to include activities that bring housekeepers into more direct contact with patients as they now draw blood, take vital signs, and help transport patients.

A salesperson is give a new assignment to help the manufacturing department discover how to incorporate more of a sales perspective in their product designs, mutual enrichment occurs. Both sales and manufacturing people start listening and learning. They all begin to see the situation in a new light. All the great teachers have recognized that lifelong learning is what fuels the soul. Michelangelo's motto was, "I am still learning." Leaders need to ask themselves whether the practice of ongoing learning is encouraged in their organization.

The Natural Instinct

As fathers of six children between us, we have been taught a lot about learning by watching our children. In their earliest years, like all children, our sons and daughters displayed an intense curiosity in reaching out to discover the world and their own capacities. It was endlessly fascinating to watch them testing the limits of every object that could be banged, moved, scraped, or chewed. Each moment and each task was given their full attention, embraced without longing for something grander. Learning included a passion for mastery, of exploring, and unfolding their inner powers.

The behavior of children has much to inform us about the soul at work. In our early and most natural state, we love to learn, to master, to explore. We work until we have mastered, and then we want to extend that mastery again. We encounter each moment fully, reaping joy even in the simplest task.

The Path of Craft is about recovering these natural instincts—the desire for mastery, the focused attention and to detail, and the immersion of self in the present moment of work. If we are to awaken the Corporate Soul, we must begin to create workplaces where people can extend their capabilities, where discovering of the love of our hands is respected, and where all of us—like young children—are able to move out of time and into the present moment.

Some Ways to Get Started on the Path of Craft

1. What tasks and activities bring out your best? These can help determine your love of hands. Now ask how you can do more of that in your present job.
2. Provide a development program that gets staff looking at what their skills and passions are. Help them take responsibility for bringing these into their work.
3. Identify a new skill/area of expertise you'd like to explore. Find a project that brings you into a new arena. Constantly look for ways to give staff the opportunity to do the same. One simple way to do this is to have people trade jobs!
4. Give more feedback to your colleagues and to those who report to you. When you see their eyes sparkle, let them know. When you see their eyes grow dim, mirror this as well. At times, crank up the courage to say, "I don't think this is your craft!"
5. Find ways to bring artistic excellence to your work. Help staff identify ways to bring more artistry to daily work. Raise the standards or, even better, have your people identify how to foster greater excellence. Discover new ways to attend to details.
6. Find a way to get workers involved in new areas of mastery where even they might be surprised at their capability. What is the equivalent of coal miner's running the pension fund in your organization?

Exercise: Assessing Progress on the Path of Craft

The following questions allow for an initial assessment of the progress you and your organization have already made on this path. The assessment is meant to guide your exploration, as opposed to provide some definitive quantitative assessment of the state of your Corporate Soul.

Answer each question as to how true this is of you in your present work situation and then for your company.

1 = strongly agree
2 = agree
3 = disagree
4 = strongly disagree

____ In my present work I frequently lose track of time.

____ I look for ways to raise the level of artistry in the tasks I am doing.

____ My present job feels like the love of my hands.

____ When I find myself drifting off, I do things to bring myself into the moment.

____ Our company has a method in place for staff to assess their skills and interests.

____ In our company people get new assignments that are out of the box from their current capabilities (at all levels).

____ In our company we pay attention to details.

Individual Reflection & Action

Using the previous assessment, what are some actions you could take right away to begin to tread more fully the path of self in your work? Try to identify two actions to get you started as opposed to a large number that will not be implemented.

_____

_____

_____

_____

Group Reflection & Action

If your whole leadership team is reading the book, use the mini-assessment and questions as a group. As is the case with all change, begin with a few manageable ideas you can and will take action on.

_____

_____

_____

_____

_____

Exercise: Soul in the Moment

Reflect for a few minutes on the daily activities in your present work. What it would mean to treat each of those activities as if they were sacred? How might you perform them differently or view them differently if you recognized that Corporate Soul only emerges in such daily tasks?

_____

_____

_____

_____

_____

_____

Exercise: The Love of Your Hands

Think back on a project or assignment where you
felt like your soul was engaged. What tasks were you
actually doing?

_____

_____

_____

_____

_____

_____

_____

What was appealing about those tasks?

_____

_____

_____

_____

_____

_____

_____

Another way to access the love of our hands is to make a list of all the activities you do in your current job (talking to customers on the telephone to resolve problems, writing manuals, leading meetings, and so forth). After you have made a list, rate each task in terms of how much you have a sense of losing track of time and become naturally engaged while doing that activity.

_____

_____

_____

_____

_____

_____

"The fundamental delusion of humanity is to suppose that I am here and you are out there."
—Yasutani Roshi

"All is rooted in reciprocity." —Sri Yukteswar

7

The Path of Community: Why Team-Building Won't Save Your Company

Victor Coal and Lumber is a family-owned and -operated business in its third generation. Eric's grandfather-in-law, Roger Johnson, began the enterprise building large wooden water tanks more than fifty years ago. The next generation expanded into the lumber and coal business. Today, the founder's grandson supplies developers, contractors, and homeowners with everything from roof beams to lawn chairs.

Within the family, this three-generation-old business has always been referred to as simply "the store."

All the employees and most of the customers come from the surrounding small towns. A typical transaction at the store includes equal parts business and small talk—weather, crops, and news of family and friends. In a small-town business such as this, it is easy to see the multiple connections that run between work, family, and the community at large. It is easy to feel a social intimacy that is grounded more in human than economic terms. The store is part of a community, and there is community within the store.

Sharing Common Ground

When your neighbors grow the food that you buy and provide the services you require, when you know the children and the parents of your banker and barber, the nature of your relationships deepens. It is easy to see how you are connected to others in ways that stretch beyond commercial measurements. The sense of fellowship and mutual support that grows in such an environment is a soulful one. People who live in this kind of community speak of having roots.

This sense of roots, with all the implications of sharing common ground, of being connected in a living way, is often absent in the corporate environment. Instead of common ground there can be an emphasis on the personal agenda—building one's career and furthering one's own case—that promotes an undertone of separateness and competition. As this separateness deepens, relationships can become all business. When this happens, we disappear as persons, and our connection to others loses the quality that Martin Buber, renowned Jewish philosopher, called "meeting"—in which we mutually acknowledge each other into the fullness of our being.

In our interviews, people spoke about their soulful work experiences as times when their connection with others went deeper than business. The *Path of Community* is a way of developing these deeper connections with our work companions so that human dignity blossoms.

Following the Path of Community cultivates a new level of honesty in communication and a new vision of collaboration between individuals, work units, suppliers, distributors, and the community at large. True community is a powerful force that calls forth the best from people.

Everybody's Doing It

Teams, team building, and team organizations are everywhere. The belief that when people work together more effectively, the organization will achieve more of what it wants, has generated a national team fever. Some of these team efforts have produced positive results but many have produced disappointment. As one Fortune 100 manager said to us about a project implementing self-managed teams, "Doing teams here is like celebrating mass at a Mafia retreat. It looks good but its not likely to make a difference." He was concerned that team building in his company had become an empty ritual. "It's something we all go through. We know what words to say, what moves to make. But basically we aren't changing." This manager is not alone in his experience. Empty rituals take place daily in meeting rooms across the country.

In our public seminars we ask how many people belong to organizations that are engaged in some form of "team" effort. Ninety percent of the hands go up. Then we ask, "What does it mean in your organization when someone says, 'Be a team player?'" We get a range of responses from "Be a team player means 'You aren't focused on the customer'" to "Be a team player means 'Just shut up and do what I want.'" When the team concept is used as a weapon for stifling individual thought and expression, cynicism blossoms. Team building does not have to be an empty ritual. It can be a doorway to community. The Path of Community takes team building from a superficial ritual to a living experience that changes how people think about their work relationships and how they work together.

The Path of Community is based on the realization that a fundamental interdependence underlies everything we do. Every service rendered or product delivered is the result of an incalculable cooperative effort. We really are in this together.

On the Path of Community we support others because we know success is only possible through collective effort. We recognize it is impossible to shine in a vacuum. As Rumi says, "Your lamp was lit from another lamp." Everything we do rests on the efforts of others.

Learning What It Means to Have Community

We learn about love and relationships from our earliest experiences. How our parents related to us and to each other shapes our view of what love should and can be. So, too, we learn about the meaning of community from the work places we enter, especially early in our careers. One such early experience for John helped shape his view of community at work and serves as a model for this path.

When John first entered the field of organizational consulting he worked with twelve other people nestled in the midst of a government bureaucracy. They were the Organization Effectiveness Program (OEP) for the city of San Diego. Although he had worked on teams before, this experience was different. The OEP went beyond the traditional notion of teams; it was a true community. The department was the envy of the fifty-odd departments residing in the government building. The intensity of spirit, the level of service, the accomplishments, the creativity, and the amount of laughter was remarkable.

What made this group into such a community and why did it produce such stellar work? To start with, the boundary between professional and personal was blurred in a way that strengthened authentic interdependence. Community members knew each other's goals—personally and professionally—and pushed each other to clarify those goals when they were unfocused.

There was a sense of underlying support manifest as challenging feedback and praise that was lavish and heartfelt. Although praise was frequent, there was a healthy "B.S. meter," which filtered out sugar-coated criticism or false compliments.

Feedback was constant—good, bad, and everything in between. There was a commitment to growth and everyone expected everyone else to grow. Thriving in such an environment called for a lively mix of intensity, honesty, and humor. In an environment where your cherished image of yourself might be challenged at any moment, a sense of humor was required. In the atmosphere of honesty and feedback, people rapidly learned that how we see ourselves is not always the way we come across.

Rituals that reinforced the sense of community ranged from the serious to the ridiculous. But whether silly or sublime, excellence and full participation were the norm. For example, there was a tradition in which each team member wrote a poem for the member celebrating his or her birthday. That meant receiving twelve birthday poems, again ranging from the profound to the hilarious. But if the poem writing was done with little thought, the lazy author paid the price with public jibes.

Many times in his two years as a member of that work community, John received feedback that nearly brought him to tears. The feedback was rarely off target and was always aimed at making him better. The OEP had the reputation for being a "mutual admiration society." In fact, people in this work community did admire each other. And the depth of that admiration made anything less than honest feedback impossible.

Reflecting on this singular experience suggests a model for community at work. Community is nurtured when people know each other's stories (their hopes, their fears, their goals for work life). Community is fostered when feedback is truly inherent in the corporate culture, when we tell each other, with compassion, what must be known if we are to mature and grow. Community profoundly influences performance when truth is spoken without fear and the whole organization moves forward as a result.

A Place of Stories

One of the hallmarks of an organization treading the Path of Community is that people share their stories and learn to acknowledge each other for more than results. Community building starts as we expand our acknowledgment of others from "what you do" to "who you are." In community we seek to meet the person who carries the role, title, and responsibility of a particular job, as illustrated in the following Zen tale.

The governor of Kyoto came to visit a great Zen master. The attendant presented the card of the governor, which read: *Kitagaki, Governor of Kyoto.*

Glancing at the card, the master said, "I have no business with such a fellow. Tell him to get out of here."

The attendant returned the card with apologies.

"That was my error," said the governor and taking a pencil he firmly crossed out the words *Governor of Kyoto.* "Ask your master again."

"Oh, is it Kitagaki?" exclaimed the teacher. "I want to see that fellow."

The Path of Community opens us to see how a person is infinitely more than his or her job. We see the rich, complex, and many layered tapestry that is the other's individual life. In his book, *Leadership as an Art,* Max Dupree tells of a condolence call he paid to the widow of a longtime factory worker. Dupree describes the revelation that occurred when the widow read from a poetry collection that the employee had written. He realized there is so much richness within each person waiting to be discovered. And until it is discovered it will be forever excluded from the workplace.

Attending the annual picnic at a client company we watched as hundreds of people danced to the blues stylings of a band featuring the vice president of engineering, an administrative assistant, a lab technician, and two members of the building maintenance crew. We saw the amazing passion, talent, and life that was within those performers; we glimpsed the expansive dimensions of their soul. The Path of Community is built on moments of vision like this when we see past the limits of our roles and peek into the depths of the soul.

Such a vision shifts us from defining others in terms of our own agenda or a job title to recognizing the inherent value of each person. Rather than evaluating others in terms of their functional value, we allow ourselves to be touched by their essential value.

To be a member of a community is not simply to fulfill a role but to be known as a living soul. To become a member of a community calls on one to be vulnerable, to having others know one's greatness and one's weakness. In building community we put more than our competency on the table; we also put our heart, dreams, history, and values there.

Expectations of performance are not lowered when we see into the other's soul. Rather, there is a realization of how much more each of us has to offer. It becomes irresponsible not to remind each other of the greatness that is being held inside. The more we know and are connected to people, the more we will work hard to support their success.

Listening for the Sacred Within Others

In our years of consulting experience we have yet to encounter a company that did not want to improve its communication. Leaders hope that by improving the clarity of communication organizational performance will be enhanced. Yet "poor" communication thrives in a soil of separateness where people see each other as nothing but their function. Communication works when it arises from a sense of commitment and interdependence.

No listening technique can overcome a lack of appreciation. Conversely, if we really see another person as valuable, we will naturally be inclined to listen to them. Communication skills alone are not enough. Communication skills are the flowers that grow in the soil of community. Make rich community soil first and the flower of communication has a basis for growing.

Deepening the Conversation

One can sense the depth of community in the depth of the conversations that take place. Do people at your work talk about their passions, dreams, and goals? Are they giving each other truthful feedback? Is there room in the organization for truth to be spoken? If we are interested in awakening the Corporate Soul we need to create communities that promote deeper forms of communication. The alchemical process that transforms a mere collection of individuals into a soulful community is not automatic.

The best way to begin this process is to do so directly. Take time in the meetings of a company to have a true "meeting" to learn about and acknowledge each other. Learn about educational and professional backgrounds, about family history and personal goals. Learn about the dreams and values that motivate individuals and explore appropriate ways of supporting them in achieving their visions. In this way the context of work relationship shifts from "I need you to perform this task" to "I support you in your life."

Another way that we have found to be of use is to take time for people to speak about the following:

- What they love about their work
- A person they admire and why
- What gives them the greatest sense of fulfillment at work and outside work
- What they would do if they did not have to work for money

Such exercises give people a way of starting community conversation and indicating that "who we are" is important.

What We Can't Talk About

What we can't or don't talk about in an organization is often as important as what we talk about. At a management retreat a team was discussing an issue that involved their company's relationship with a governmental agency and a group of key customers. It was a tough issue and the team began to devise a strategy for addressing it. Stan, the vice president of finance, spoke up: "I think we need to ask ourselves how this strategy jives with the values and vision we have been talking about for the past eight months." In fact, this organization had recently unveiled a new values and vision statement to all its employees. Like many such statements it was lofty and ambitious. "Well, what do you think?" he asked. No one said anything for a few moments. It was clear the strategy they were developing was in direct conflict with their espoused values and stated vision. The vice president's question opened the team to a new level of conversation that challenged them to look more closely at how their beliefs were reflected in their actions.

In every group there are certain ideas, topics, and issues that are off limits. These have been called the "unmentionables." The specific content of these unmentionables will vary from organization to organization, but they are always charged with emotion. There are few more potent ways of liberating collective energy and awakening Corporate Soul than to uncover and transform an organization's unmentionables. After telling our personal stories, talking about unmentionables takes the Path of Community to the next level.

In traditional team-building, people develop ground rules as a way of shaping team behavior. But establishing ground rules, no matter how valid they are, will rarely catalyze the inner shift needed to move people forward on the Path of Community. That requires paying attention to the inner life of the group, the unmentionable underground rules, those unconscious or unexamined agreements that shape behavior, define what can be discussed, and impel decision making. Only the most open community is free of underground rules. Whenever issues of power and control are present (when aren't they?), conditions are ripe for the growth of underground rules.

When we ask people to identify the underground rules that limit their ability to address critical issues, make important decisions, and take necessary actions, they are initially silent. It is in the nature of underground rules that they are unmentionable. These are taboo subjects that can only be grumbled about around the water cooler or in the bar after hours, not discussed in an open forum! Putting underground rules on the table, simply and directly, is often frightening at first. But once a group learns it can safely explore its own inner life, the fear of naming the underground rules dissolves.

It takes courage to start the process. When Stan challenged his peer's decision because it ran counter to the espoused corporate values, he was challenging an underground rule that could be stated as "values are for presenting but not necessarily for living."

Rewriting Underground Rules

It is the unspoken and unexamined nature of the underground rules that give them their power. Like Dorothy in the *Wizard of Oz* we have been told to "ignore that man behind the curtain!" But as long as an underground rule is hidden from view it maintains its invisible power to shape a team or company's destiny.

Some of the underground rules groups have identified for us include:

- You don't have to do what you say.
- Don't talk about your real passion; pretend your

current job is your dream.

- Only the boss can decide (but we act like we reach consensus).
- It's okay to be absent mentally as long as you sit quietly.
- Don't confront each other; just work around each other.
- Don't mention the "pet" project.
- Do not give each other direct feedback about managerial behavior.
- Talk only about numbers not how we work together.

Viewed in isolation such rules seem patently ridiculous. Yet underground rules develop for a purpose. They invariably turn out to be cumbersome and unskillful ways of trying to make things go smoothly for a group.

We worked with a management team whose underground rules—"Don't confront"—had the positive intent of minimizing harmful personal attacks but with the limiting side effect of discouraging any open expression of differences.

This team's unspoken agreement to protect each other from confrontation ultimately led to enormous friction between the members. With no open forum for giving feedback, tensions grew and factions developed. It was cold war. All people wanted to do at one point was confront each other. "Let's just get a bunch of baseball bats and go in a room and get this out of our systems," was one team member's suggestion. Such is the result of following underground rules to their bizarre conclusion.

Finding the Positive Intention

Even the most intelligent groups fall into self-limiting behaviors. Transforming restrictive underground rules requires that we respect and preserve what is positive about these rules while at the same time eliminating their detrimental side effects. For the management team mentioned above, this meant talking about their fears of confrontation and developing useful agreements about how to give and receive feedback.

Overturning underground rules can release tremendous pent-up energy within a group. Time, effort, and emotional resources restricted or distorted by underground rules are now available for constructive purposes. Rewriting underground rules allows a group to stare into a collective mirror, to see themselves, and to choose more productive and fulfilling ways of interacting.

We follow three steps when transforming underground rules:

1. Identify the limiting rule. This is done by asking, "If there were a rule limiting us what would it be?"
2. Clarify both the positive intent of the underground rule and the negative side effects. All underground rules arise from some positive intent. Unfortunately, their negative side effects are much worse. Seeing both prepares a group for change.
3. Agree to a new rule that preserves the positive intent and moves the group forward.

Awakening Corporate Soul

Communities as a House of Mirrors

As children growing up in New York City, we used to go across the river to Palisades Amusement Park in New Jersey. One of our favorite amusements was the house of mirrors, a large mirror-walled maze in which a child could get playfully lost. Everywhere you looked, there you were. A house of mirrors is an apt metaphor for community at work, a place where others help us see ourselves.

When growth is nurtured through the giving and receiving of honest feedback rooted in a mutual desire for excellence, community blossoms. We ground our feedback in the attitude of compassion, holding the vision of others' greatness before our inner eye. Along with a greater commitment to honestly giving others feedback comes a readiness to open our heart to feedback from others.

In Buddhism this practice is called "loving kindness," a method for moving our mind and heart beyond any intention to blame or harm. Instead we develop the powerful intention that others might truly realize their inner greatness. This is accomplished by holding three thoughts:

- May you be free from fear.
- May you be filled with well being.
- May you awaken in loving kindness.

As we absorb these three thoughts fully they become the foundation of our communication. Then all our words will be words of awakening. Even challenging feedback can be delivered in the spirit of loving kindness.

The ability to cut through delusions and communicate compassionately is an art. The ability to hear critical feedback without becoming defensive is an even higher art. Working toward this is exactly what builds community. If our hearts open enough with loving kindness, then it is possible to develop mutual support to a very high degree. The great Sufi saint Rumi described this state of mutual support perfectly when he wrote, "Out beyond ideas of right doing and wrong doing there is a field. I'll meet you there."

The development of such an organizational milieu is the aim of the Path of Community. This requires inner work as well as open communication. Cultivating loving kindness within ourselves builds our capacity to change work relationships that have become stuck.

Transforming Adversaries Through Loving Kindness

Elizabeth, the manager of a large information systems department, worked closely with her general manager designing a new technology strategy and developing a budget to fund the new investment. But every conversation was like a battle. "I began to see him as my enemy," she said. " And I decided he was nothing more than a narrow-minded power glutton."

In her mind the general manager became a caricature of the "evil boss" and she became by necessity the caricature of the "downtrodden victim." She explained, "I really saw myself as a voice crying out in a barren wilderness. And the wilderness was his mind."

After learning the loving kindness practice, Elizabeth decided to give it a try. Each evening before falling asleep she would visualize the general manager and mentally say, "May you be free from fear. May you be filled with well being. May you awaken in loving kindness."

It was not easy. "I found I had immense inner resistance to doing the loving kindness practice. I was really invested in his being the bad guy," she admitted. But she kept at it. Then driving to work for an early morning meeting, her awareness of the situation shifted.

"My mind began to automatically run through the practice. I was effortlessly sending him the three thoughts. Then I began to see my boss as he is in the rest of his life. I saw him at home, interacting with his kids. Next, I began to see him as a young boy, as a student. I saw an entire movie of his life. And even though I knew most of it was coming from my imagination, I began to feel differently. I saw him as a person on his own path, with his own struggles, and I really felt loving kindness," she continued. "I walked into the meeting with the awareness that he was more than 'my boss;' he was a person. I still did not agree with many of his positions, but that no longer meant I had to judge him personally. Things between us became easy from then on."

By seeing her boss as more than a bullying authority Elizabeth was able to free herself from the trap of being the "long-suffering and misunderstood genius." Grounded in loving kindness and a fuller sense of his humanity she was able to open up a new way of being for herself and a new way of communicating with him.

Through the practice of loving kindness, Elizabeth found that inner transformation and outer change walk hand in hand on the Path of Community. As the yoga master Sri Yukteswar said, "All is rooted in reciprocity." When we change our inner landscape the outer world changes too.

Beyond the We-They Syndrome

In hierarchical organizations the Path of Community involves dissolving the walls that separate people at one level of the organization from those at another. To dissolve barriers is both an inner action, as demonstrated by Elizabeth's application of loving kindness to her "ogre" of a boss—and an outer action—when leaders model vulnerability.

We witnessed the power of leadership vulnerability at a large hospital facing a traumatic reorganization process. The senior vice president was at a meeting with frontline employees who were bitter and upset about the changes in their jobs and the new "soulless attitude" that was taking over the institution. One outspoken staff member stood up and said in a shaky voice, "Not a day goes by when I don't want to come in and say, 'I quit.' But I can't." Many heads nodded in agreement but no one else spoke. There was a sense of anger and frustration in the room. All eyes turned toward the vice president, awaiting her response. She paused for what seemed like minutes and then said quietly, "It's the same for me." The silence that followed was deeper. The vulnerability of a leader, who put her truth on the table rather than offer an explanation, created a moment of connection that led everyone away from complaining to mutual problem solving.

Community cuts across all lines of status and function and manifests itself in myriad ways. It is when an executive regularly takes a "walk in the shoes" of front-line employees by working next to them. It is the after-hours sports teams that have people from across the organization playing together. It is the CEO who occasionally has lunch with someone far down the "ladder," not as some show of grace but as an acceptable form of friendship nurtured within the company. It is when the company's books are open for all to see. If we are to be a community we must have access to the same information. However manifested, community building is always about removing barriers and creating connections between and among people.

Not Everyone Belongs Here

In this time of political correctness it is not always acceptable to recognize people are different. But people who thrive in one culture are not the same as those who thrive in another. Some people will fit better and be more apt to find community in some organizations than in others. Although it is unmentionable in most circles, there is such a thing as "our kind of people."

It is important to recognize what kind of an organization we have and help people figure out up front if this is the kind of place they can find community. Some people could never have found community in the poem-writing, free-wheeling feedback climate of John's OEP city of San Diego team. John vividly recalls a new team member who was "rejected" by the team. He was bright and quite talented but needed a different environment for his talents to be recognized. When we worked with a division of Pepsi, it was obvious to us if not to them that competitive sports-minded managers fit in better in that community. There is a culture in your company and not everyone will find community in it.

One organization we worked with actually went through a process to identify what "we are like around here." They created a videotape for prospective employees describing their culture. Applicants could make an educated choice about their "fit" with the organization.

The Net of Jewels

An image from India called the Net of Jewels beautifully describes the reciprocity that the Path of Community embodies. In this image each being in the universe (whether person, plant, animal, or angel) is envisioned to be a perfect jewel. All these jewels are seen as linked together in an intricate weblike pattern, much like a universal fishing net. A jewel resides at each node of the net.

And every jewel, because of its crystalline integrity reflects within itself a perfect image of the whole net. Thus, the total net is reflected an infinite number of times in each of the jewels that stretch from one end of the universe to the other. In this way, every jewel of the net is present in every other jewel, and the net as a whole is present in each jewel. Individuality and interdependence coexist in absolute balance.

In Hinduism and Buddhism this image is used to articulate the profound way in which we participate in the life of the universe. We are not isolated actors. We do not live in a mechanistic universe where people are like billiard balls, fundamentally separate from each other; where "relationships" are the result of billiard balls colliding into one another, bouncing around in reaction.

Rather, the Net of Jewels suggests we are coparticipants in a living community that is rooted in total interdependence. As the naturalist John Muir observed, "When we pick out anything by itself, we find it hitched to everything else in the universe."

Freedom From Victimization

This vision of interdependence can be frustrating to the part of us that wants to be either a victim or a dictator. Both are billiard-ball ways of thinking: Victims believe, "They are rolling into me and making me bounce around like this." Dictators believe, "I can control others."

Awakening to interdependence means rethinking our "billiard ball" notions of power and influence. In a truly interdependent universe leadership is ubiquitous; every part of the whole is constantly influencing every other part.

As the Corporate Soul awakens we see more and more the interdependent nature of life and transform our concepts of power and control. We give up the fantasy that those "above us" are the bigger billiard balls who are "in charge."

We see that adopting the attitude of the victim is a self-imposed illusion. And, we see that as apparently frustrating as victimization can be, it is also a comforting dream, lulling us into dependency. As victims we can believe we are helpless; we can believe it's "not my fault."

Interdependence, which is the heart of community, invites us to step into a world where no individual is "in control." As we enter the soulful community, control is replaced with cocreating. Of all human needs, the need to connect is one of the strongest. That is why a child deprived of touch will eventually die. As our companies become places of true "meeting," we connect with each other and jointly awaken the Corporate Soul.

Some Ways to Get Started on the Path of Community

1. Plan ways for people to get to know each other beyond their function.
2. Find ways to break down the we-they syndrome: Have leaders do a regular rotation "walking in the shoes" of front-line staff; let them get out to where the real work is being done.
3. Mention the "unmentionable" rules in your team or company. As leaders, encourage discussion of the unmentionables!
4. Open the books and share information that normally would be held in confidence (financial reports, salaries, and so on).
5. Share your story in personal ways—why you love what you do, what you love to do when not at work, what you want your legacy to be.
6. Identify the "kind of people" who thrive in your company and become more clear about this in your hiring process.

Exercise: Polishing Your Own House of Mirrors

1. Find someone from whom you would value some genuine heart-to-heart honesty concerning how you are at work. Make it a person whose intentions you trust, not an adversary who would see this as an opportunity to slay you. Write down the questions you'd hope they'd answer. Think of the areas in which you would like feedback, such as, "How good am I at handling conflict?" Then arrange a time to sit down and hear them out. Put your defensive shield down and go with a genuine desire to hear.

_____

_____

_____

_____

_____

_____

_____

_____

_____

2. Find someone in the organization you think would benefit from your feedback. Make sure you are steeped in an intention of kindness and helpfulness going in. Share things that would be of help to them, even if they are things they have not heard before.

_____

_____

_____

_____

_____

_____

_____

_____

_____

Exercise: Assessing Progress on the Path of Community

The questions below allow for an initial assessment of the progress you and your organization have already made on this path. The assessment is meant to guide your exploration, as opposed to providing some definitive quantitative assessment of the state of your Corporate Soul.

For each question below, answer as to how true this is of you in your present work situation or your company.

1 = strongly agree
2 = agree
3 = disagree
4 = strongly disagree

___ In my present work I give other people a great deal of genuine feedback aimed at their development.
___ I share information on my own goals and personal passions with my colleagues.
___ I frequently challenge the community stifling power of the "unmentionables" by saying what is really true
___ As a leader, I do many activities that get me closer to those I lead.
___ I welcome feedback aimed at my growth.
___ Our company is a feedback-rich environment.

___ Leaders are approachable, vulnerable, and accessible

___ In our company people frequently have opportunities to share their story and to socialize in ways that build genuine community.

___ Our company has an environment where there are few unmentionables.

___ At our company, the front-line know as much about what is actually going on as the people at the top.

Reflection

Based on the previous responses, what are the areas of potential growth for you? What about your company? In the areas of greatest opportunity, identify an example or two that shows how you know growth is needed.

_____

_____

_____

_____

_____

_____

_____

_____

_____

_____

Take the time now to reflect on what you have read about this path. Using the assessment above, what are some actions you could take right away to begin to tread more fully the path of self in your work? Try to identify two actions to get you started as opposed to a large number that will not be implemented.

_____

_____

_____

_____

_____

_____

_____

_____

_____

_____

_____

Group Reflection & Action

If your whole leadership team is reading the book, use the mini-assessment above and work as a group on the questions below. As always, we have offered some ideas on ways to get started. As is the case with all change, begin with a manageable few that you can and will take action on.

_____

_____

_____

_____

_____

_____

_____

_____

_____

_____

_____

_____

"Wake up,
Wake up,
and clothe yourself with strength."
—Isaiah 52:1

"You must be the change you want to see in the world."
—Gandhi

8

The Leader's Soul:
You Can't Lead Others
Where You Haven't Been

Theologian Henri Nouwen succinctly stated, "The great illusion of leadership is to think that a man can be led out of the desert by someone who has never been there." Awakening Corporate Soul requires a new kind of leadership. The watchwords for leaders of Corporate Soul are, "Go where you would lead." It is important that leaders have familiarity with the terrain they are encouraging others to travel.

Get Personal Experience on the Paths

Those who would lead others will need to spend time:

- on the Path of Self, probing their own inner depths and surfacing their own sacred values,
- on the Path of Contribution, identifying the higher purpose of their work,
- on the Path of Craft, engaging in a process of mastery and learning, and
- on the Path of Community, connecting deeply with others.

It is this basis of personal experience that gives rise to credible leadership.

To attempt to lead others into the unfamiliar territory of Corporate Soul without first having made the trek oneself is to fall into a hollow kind of preaching. One may say all the right words: empowerment, heart, vision, purpose, community, values, and so forth. But if the words are not rooted in one's own experience of walking (and perhaps stumbling) upon the paths, then even the most eloquent words sound like empty slogans. People hear the hype, not the heart, and turn away.

Not an Expert

Walking the Four Paths does not turn one into an expert. Being a leader is different from being an expert. There are no experts with fool proof answers or pat formulas in the domain of Corporate Soul. Each journey of awakening will be unique. Every person, team, and organization will find their way. But the leader who has pursued his or her own journey can function as a guide, not because he or she knows what hides around every boulder or bend in the road, but because that leader has personally passed through similar trials.

From Answers to Awareness

One of the greatest traps of leadership is becoming an "answer machine," to be the "one who knows." Of course, our success may appear to be evidence that we have a special access to insight and answers. Leaders, like everyone, have knowledge, but overreliance on our own experience weds us to the past. We are limited by what we know. Paradoxically, we are limited by the very knowledge that has been the basis of our past success. Knowledge, which by definition is related to the past, cannot help us create the future. As long as we rely on the knowledge and answers of our past, we will be compelled to perpetuate the past.

This happens regularly in organizations when leaders proclaim a "new" organizational initiative. What appears new to the leaders is often considered by the rest of the organization to be nothing more than last year's initiative reheated. The name changes but the substance remains the same.

Leaders do not do this maliciously. They want to solve organizational problems. They want to have good answers. But this very investment in "knowing," this grasping of answers, hooks leaders into a cycle of recreating the same solution over and over. When this happens, it becomes harder to engage people in committing these initiatives. Cynicism greets the latest program.

By dropping the need to know and letting go of having to have answers, leaders can expand their horizon of awareness. They open to what the Zen masters call "beginners mind," in which new choices lead them out of the cycle of cynicism.

When Eric was in college he worked part time for Roman, a textile designer who practiced Zen meditation. When Roman was invited to lunch with a visiting Korean Zen master, he invited Eric along. Lunch took place in a room at the Buddhist temple. Four people were in attendance:, Eric, Roman, the master, and a monk. The traditional meal was taken in silence. Then the master turned to Eric's boss and, staring into his eyes, asked in broken English, "You have question?"

"How can I improve my meditation?" Roman asked.

"Improve meditation!" yelled the master. "Where is Buddha when you meditate?!" Roman stared at the master dumbfounded.

"Where is Buddha when you eat?! Where is Buddha when you go toilet?!"

"I...I don't know," Roman replied.

The master leapt to his feet smiling and opening his arms in a sweeping gesture as if clearing the space around him, shouted, "Yes!! Yes!! Don't know!! Don't know! Always keep that don't-know mind!"

What is the meaning of this Zen drama? Was the master inviting Roman to become ignorant? Hardly. Don't-know mind is Zen parlance for the mind of all possibilities. Don't-know mind is the creative mind unencumbered by the "known" and the past. Don't-know mind is the mind that leaps over yesterday's worn out strategies. Don't-know mind frees us from what author Lucy Freeman calls "terminal knowing." For as long as our attempts to improve our organizations are limited by our past we will never innovate. "Knowing" is the leader's dilemma and the don't-know mind is the doorway out. Don't-know mind is the mind of awareness not answers. Awareness opens us to the possibilities inherent in our present conditions and problems. As long as we rely on our "knowing," these possibilities are invisible. Leaders who overinvest themselves in having the right answers cannot cultivate a "don't know" mind, one that opens them to asking new questions, uncovering new insights, and taking new actions.

From Struggle to Strength

It is common for leaders who are implementing change programs to encounter "resistance" from others. Many leaders try to overcome this resistance through persuasion, coercion, or other forms of subtle or not-so-subtle manipulation. Unfortunately, all these displays of power seem only to increase the resistance or to cause it to resurface as malicious compliance. The more we pursue the paths to Corporate Soul the more we find that the major leadership challenges lie within us rather than in the environment.

One leader told us, "I can get everyone to go to quality training, but that doesn't make for quality." As long as we are committed to flexing our muscles, we will never be able to turn within and make the changes that can free us and our organizations. A one-sided commitment to overpowering our outer foes will keep us from being able to turn within and make the changes that can free us from resource-wasting power struggles.

It is remarkable how much can be accomplished by making subtle inner changes. When we truly let go of struggling against others, the possibility of dialogue appears. When we stop trying to assert our power over others, they will be able to take our words seriously.

True power is never based on our outer trappings of authority but on our inner congruence and balance. If we undertake the Corporate Soul journey as another outer conquest, all our efforts will be for naught. The journey pursued as a conquest of outer forces will actually keep us from awakening the soul. That is why Lao Tsu says, "Mastering others is force; mastering yourself is true power." Leaders who overpower others can never call forth a creative response. People will submit to pressure but only fully commit themselves to vision. Their creativity responds to the call of a higher purpose. Their compliance (sometimes vicious compliance) responds to manipulative power.

The Need to Wake Ourselves First

Powerful leaders start the journey to Corporate Soul by taking responsibility for awakening themselves first. This takes a special kind of effort.

The Zen master Zuigan used to call out to himself, "Zuigan, are you there?"

"Yes, master!"

"Are you awake?"

"Yes, master!"

"Really awake?"

"Yes, master."

"Don't be misled, confused, or sidetracked!"

Staying awake means catching ourselves being misled, confused, and sidetracked, which can occur the higher we move in the organizational structure. Senior leaders are often insulated from bad news. They can become enamored of their own achievements. They can be surrounded by people who agree with them too easily and by symbols of achievement that flatter the ego but put the soul to sleep. The higher we move in the organization, the more challenging it becomes for others to confront us, to provide straightforward feedback, and to question our ideas. This situation is deadly for the soul.

For the ego it can be enthralling to watch our own self-image becoming more and more powerful. The ego likes to be confirmed in its hunch that "I really am powerful and smart!" The wisdom traditions tell us that awakened leadership arises from a different source than ego, with its heavy investment in preserving an idealized self-image.

At the Threshold of Change

There is something enticing and compelling—and terrifying—about the possibility of awakening soul at work. This dual experience of being drawn forward and of pulling back occurs at the threshold of a major change. It is the experience of being at the crossroads. Leaders who find themselves in this condition are experiencing what mythologist Joseph Campbell refers to as hearing the call.

The journey to a new way of leadership begins with hearing the call. Having heard the call of the soul we edge toward a commitment to taking the journey of awakening. Yet as we approach the threshold and prepare to take our fist real step onto the path, we catch the smell of death and recoil.

"What," we wonder, "is this smell of death that lingers at the threshold of the path to soul?" It is the aroma of our own self-image, our small self, going up in smoke. For in order to make room for the energy of the soul, the image we have of ourselves will have to be sacrificed. It is just an image, after all, but we have invested many years and much effort building it up. It may even come with a corner office, a title, or other perks. Approaching the threshold of the path to soul is threatening to one's self-image. It's uncomfortable but inevitable, which is why the Sufi master Rumi says, "Die before you die." He is encouraging us to relinquish our self-image before life or circumstances intervene and take it from us.

Die Before You Die

How can we die before we die? In the era of downsizing and job insecurity many have found their self-image torn out from under them. "It can be very difficult," reported a downsized executive, "when your whole identity is wrapped up in the job and the activities of the job, to find a sense of self when those are gone." For many this uninvited downsizing becomes a life-transforming experience. "Once I wasn't my job title," another manager told us, "I had to find out who I was that was deeper than my business card."

It is not necessary to lose our jobs to give up our self-image. We can do so as an act of leadership. Giving up our self-image can feel more dangerous than physical death. After all, in choosing to shift the base of our power from our position to our inner being requires a radical reorientation.

"I got a certain kind of thrill out of being in charge," the CEO of a gourmet food company reported. "It was exciting to be relied on, to have answers, to be in the center of the action." This leader came to a point in his work where something more than "being in charge" was valued. "Making a change in our company required that I make a change in myself."

The Mirage of Success

The irony of all this is that our self-image is a mirage. We do thirst for something of value but have mistaken our limited self-interest for an oasis of meaning. Pursuing self-interest can bring us promotions, rewards, and accolades—all good things. But without soul and a sense of meaning they become empty symbols.

So we choose to awaken from the dream of our self-image. And rather than pursue the mirage of success, we look to those soulful leadership values that are enduring.

How We Are Limited by Our Talents

We cross the threshold from traditional leadership to soulful leadership when we see the pattern that has made us successful and see how that same pattern limits us. The talents and abilities that have taken us "this far" have become the very patterns that impede further development.

"My competitiveness has helped build this organization," the vice president of sales at a biotech firm once told us. "But this same competitiveness has isolated me from other members of the senior team. Competition worked for me in the marketplace but works against me when I can't turn it off back at the office."

Gandhi once said, "I believe the only demons worth taming are the ones inside of ourselves!" It is easier in many ways to pursue the outer demons—the forces that threaten market share, customer loyalty, and shareholder attitudes. We are on less certain ground when we turn inside to examine the forces within us that define what we can create.

Like the sales vice president quoted above, we can start by seeing those "winning" patterns of behavior that have become all-consuming habits. It may be our insistence on making all the decisions, which, while it served us in the past, now saps the energy and initiative of our people. Or perhaps it is our habit of assertively stating our viewpoint that overpowers our ability to listen thoughtfully. Seeing these behavioral patterns is useful. And the soul journey can take us even deeper.

When Jesus went to the desert to fast and purify himself, he encountered Satan. As the Buddha sat under the Bo tree, determined not to rise again until attaining full enlightenment, he encountered Mara, the king of demons. In every account of profound awakening there is the encounter with temptation. From the point of view of awakening Corporate Soul the greatest temptation is the clinging to our self-image and the goals that arise from that image. Campbell succinctly says that the hesitancy that arises at the threshold of change is in fact the refusal to "give up what one takes to be one's own interest."

Weighing Ourselves in the Balance

In ancient Egypt the souls of the departed were placed on the "scales of justice." The soul was placed on one side of the scale and a feather was placed on the other. This scale measured the weight of the soul. Was this soul heavily burdened with artificial self-images? If so, the scales tipped down. Or was the soul light as a feather having divested itself of artificiality? If so, the scales would tip up and the soul would ascend to the realms of light. Leaders don't have to wait for physical death to ask these questions or measure the authenticity of their leadership.

Abraham's Challenge

In the Old Testament Abraham is confronted with the ultimate challenge of sacrifice by God. Abraham is asked to offer his most precious creation, his son Isaac, as a sacrifice. He obeys. And at the culminating moment of absolute willingness and complete letting go, with the knife about to plunge into his son's heart, an angel comes to stay Abraham's hand. Through his willingness to sacrifice his own son, Abraham confronted and clarified his most primary values. Although this story has been interpreted in many ways, from the perspective of leadership and the Corporate Soul it speaks of the power of sacrifice.

Isaac represents whatever is most precious and whatever we would not want to sacrifice. Isaac represents the continuity of Abraham's lineage. Isaac embodies the promise that things won't change, for he will carry on the tradition. Through Isaac Abraham's leadership will continue. It all seems so organized, a neat succession of father to son, a smooth and unbroken progression from the past to the future. Abraham is being asked to determine whether he is more committed to perpetuating his past or to stepping across the threshold into a creative future. With no guarantees.

As modern Abrahams, we set goals, establish the budget, target the market, and develop the plan. We expect everything to flow forward according to schedule, but life rarely takes its cues from our strategic plan. Life, in a turbulent marketplace, is forever turning the tables on us. The more we are attached to our plan, our "Isaac," the more we will resent life's inevitable intrusions.

In the biblical story God enters as the wild card, the unexpected element that disturbs Abraham's neatly ordered program. God asks Abraham to sacrifice his dream of stable continuity. In the marketplace, life has a way of stepping in and challenging us to sacrifice the known for the unknown.

We All Have an "Isaac"

Every leader has his or her own "Isaac," his or her own beloved creation. At one level these are the talents that have allowed us to succeed in the past. We rely on these talents; we count on them, and paradoxically we are limited by them.

One manager's "Isaac" was her ability to turn disastrous situations into successes. She had a gift for entering into situations that were on the verge of destruction and making things right. She was called upon again and again by her firm to perform her "turnaround" magic. Her ability to step into chaos and wring out coherence has been richly rewarded. This manager is tremendously talented at what she does. It is just that this talent has become the limitation that defines her role and relationships with other managers at her organization. This dominant talent has been a double-edged contribution to the organization. On the one hand it has rescued some bad situations but it has also contributed to developing a management team that is dependent on being rescued.

"I see how my ability to rescue people and situations has helped perpetuate a crisis-management culture at our company," she said. "Other managers don't need to be completely accountable because they know that when things start to fall apart they can call me in. It's almost like my talent at saving the day has made them less able to lead."

Leaders who want to lead others onto the path of the soul will have to confront themselves and sacrifice their own "Isaac." The kind of sacrifices the story of Abraham points toward goes beyond the skill-building aims behind most management development programs. There is a place for skill building—it is often desperately needed. But sacrificing one's self-image to awaken to another level of leadership is something else again. This level of sacrifice is for leaders who want to lead others into the challenging arena of relinquishing their own self-limiting success strategies.

What Gets Us Across the Threshold

There is no training program that can prepare one to cross the threshold from traditional to soulful leadership. What moves us across this threshold is when our need for a new level of depth outweighs our attachment to the past.

There are no better resources than the wisdom traditions for making this choice. In a sense that is what spiritual teachings are all about—how to hear the call, have the courage to respond, and the commitment to continue listening and learning as we move through the process of awakening.

Others will sense the quality of our inner commitment. Whether it is called "walking the talk" or "being real," there is a quality that is undeniably present in those who have smelled their self-image going up in smoke and have chosen to advance across the threshold of change in any case. Such a choice always follows a process of deep self-reflection and what Jung called "a re-evaluation of earlier values." We exchange the apparent security and certainty of our self-image for a journey that is wide open and truly creative. And we take up a new mantle of leadership based on respect, learning, and openness.

A monk asked Abba Poemen, "Some brothers live with me; do you want me to be in charge of them?"

The old man said to him, "No, just work on yourself first and foremost, and if they want to live like you, they will see to it themselves."

"But it is they themselves, Abba, who want me to be in charge of them."

"No, be their example, not their legislator."

In the end it is not our techniques that matter, it is our being. It is not our talents or our knowledge, it is our being.

Trading in our techniques, talents, and knowledge can seem like a lot to ask. The wisdom traditions all tell us that is the price for gaining the key to the soul. When we open that treasure chest we find like the Quaker author, "Deep within us there is an amazing inner sanctuary of the soul, a holy place, a divine center, a speaking voice, to which we may continuously return."

Fearlessness

The most fearless acts of leadership are those that make us most vulnerable. In the 1950s, years after World War II was over, a number of Japanese soldiers were discovered in the jungles of remote Pacific islands. These soldiers had been separated from their troops and gone into hiding to avoid capture. They never heard the news that the war was over and so had continued their strategy of self-protection. Even when they were informed, it was hard for them to accept that the war they were fighting was only in their minds.

Many of the ways leaders protect themselves are as outmoded as the strategies of those Japanese fighters. Many of the enemies we think we face are no more than projections of our fears. It is time for leaders to let go of the strategy of self-protection. Our organizations need leaders who are awake and who actively serve the emerging needs of the Corporate Soul.

Exercise: A Ritual of Crossing the Threshold

Imagine you were to cross the threshold into a new way of leading and being. What aspects of your personality, behavior, and leadership style will you have to let go of?

_____

_____

_____

_____

_____

_____

_____

With what will they be replaced?

_____

_____

_____

_____

_____

Exercise: Who Can Lead the Corporate Soul?

Write a job description for a leader of Corporate Soul (for example, responsible for modeling vulnerability, speaking personal truth, listening deeply and articulating what is below the surface, letting go of outmoded forms, and so forth).

_____

_____

_____

_____

_____

_____

_____

_____

_____

_____

_____

_____

_____

"As you go the way of life, you will see a great chasm.
Jump! It is not as wide as you think."
—Native American saying

"We must learn to reawaken and keep ourselves awake,
not by mechanical aids, but by
an infinite expectation of the dawn,
which does not forsake us even in our soundest sleep."
—Henry David Thoreau

9

Getting On the Path to Corporate Soul: Turning Obstacles Into Energy

As a child, John lived on Staten Island, just a ferry ride away from Manhattan. Many of his earliest memories involve riding the ferry across the harbor past the Statue of Liberty.

Once, in his college years, he had an interview for a great summer job in Manhattan. Getting to the interview on time meant catching a 1 P.M. ferry. Driving to the docks, John realized he had barely enough time and sped all the way. He rushed to park the car and ran to catch the boat. As he got within sight of the boat, the gate began to lift indicating it would soon depart. When he arrived at the dock, panting and sweating, the boat-man put his hand out. "Sorry, buddy, this one is on its way, there will be another in an hour!"

Dejected and with the interview for his summer job now history, John sat on a curb to bemoan his fate. A homeless man sat a few yards away looking at John with a strange look on his face. "Missed your boat, eh?" he joked.

"Uh huh," John replied with resignation. "I should have driven faster."

Without hesitation the man countered, "You should have started sooner!"

The Danger of Waiting

How many times have we started "too late," delaying the initiation of a project, putting off a phone call, procrastinating, only to discover that when we finally make our move the clock has run out?

The wisdom traditions point out that there is a tremendous urgency to our lives—a need to sow while there is daylight. However, they also say that there is no urgency. The universe has work to be done and it will get done with or without our conscious involvement. In the words of the Zen poet, "Sitting quietly, doing nothing, Spring comes."

It is by acknowledging this paradox that this book must end. On the one hand, the Corporate Soul will wake up without your help. On the other hand, there is an urgency to take action and actively participate in that awakening lest it pass your organization by.

Spiritual urgency and divine relaxation are two sides of a single coin. These attitudes are not mutually exclusive but paradoxically coexist in the present moment. In order to awaken the Corporate Soul we must learn to balance ourselves between urgency and stillness.

Too much urgency turns our efforts compulsive; we are active but not productive. Too much stillness becomes inertia and our sense of inner quiet descends into dullness. The Buddha compared the tension between urgency and relaxation to the tension in the string of a musical instrument. Music requires the string to be neither too tight nor too loose. Overdoing either extreme puts the instrument out of tune. Only when the tension is balanced can the instrument play in tune.

When we find our own balance, then we act from a place where urgency and relaxation fuse into spiritual power. And as Meister Eckhart has pointed out, spiritual power is released only in the present moment, the eternal now.

When our soul is tuned to the balance between urgency and relaxation, each moment becomes a moment of awakening. We do what needs to be done and at the same time sit back, marveling at the unexpected miracles that are unfolding around us. We are the actor, involved and passionate, and the witness, observing and detached. The doer and the watcher on the hill.

If Not Now, When?

When the Zen master Dogen traveled to China to study Buddhism, one of his greatest teachers turned out to be the monastery cook. This cook was an old man who amazed Dogen with the energy he poured into his work. Dogen asked why he never used any assistants.

"Other people are not me, " the cook answered.

Dogen agreed but questioned further, "Why are you working so hard in the hot sun?"

The cook replied, "If I do not do it now, when else can I do it?"

Many of us dream about creating a more spiritually hospitable workplace but procrastinate hoping that someone else will make the first move and begin the process of transforming the organization. Some of us bide our time hoping for conditions to become "right." Others make tentative forays but hold back waiting for permission from others before fully committing to the path of awakening. To all of us the words of the aged cook still ring true: For if we do not do it now, when else is there to act?

To ignore the imperative in this now-moment is not simply to postpone action. It is to act as if tomorrow were within our control. Like an adolescent driver playing chicken, we act as though we will live forever. Carlos Castenda's teacher Don Juan instructed him to "keep death as an advisor." In Ecclesiastes it is written, "Death is the destiny of everyone, the living should take this to heart."

Death is a good advisor for those of us who hesitate. To gaze at our own mortality without looking away can dissolve procrastination in a flash. Death, like the old Buddhist cook, reminds us that life is only guaranteed for this moment. If we don't act now, then when can we act?

If your work life ended today or your company ceased to exist today, what would you want to be said about the soul that was present in your company? Your leadership? Your work? Although it may sound unusual, a bit of reflection on the end of your career or the legacy of your company can provide useful lessons for today's action.

Getting Started

As this book ends, it creates a sense of spiritual urgency for us, the authors. How can we communicate so that you will take the message of Corporate Soul to heart? How can we communicate so you will find, for yourself and for your organization the energy to enter more deeply onto the soul's path? In our view, this last chapter is both about how to get started in bringing more soul to your work and your workplace, and the dragons that might keep you from even trying.

The task in this final chapter is to help you tune your instrument so you can unequivocally move forward on the path of awakening and begin to infuse your work and your corporate culture with deeper commitment and soul. Where the path of soul will take you in the end is still uncertain. The task now is to crystallize your first steps, to make the present moment—the now—a moment of soulful action.

The Corporate Soul, like a sleeping giant, is awakening. There are signs everywhere obvious to those who are already even slightly awake. What is important, at this moment, is not whether or not any of us has fully awakened. We haven't. The question is whether you are taking the next step on the path.

The First Steps Are the Most Difficult

There is a tale of a meditation master in Tibet who went on retreat for three years. In the midst of the retreat he had a vision of his deceased teacher.

"Oh, great teacher," he said, "please aid me to move forward swiftly on the path. Aid me to truly awaken, that I might aid others to awaken."

Referring to this vision, he said, "From that day forward, my teacher has always been beside me. I can hear him repeating in solemn tones whenever I begin to lose the path: 'Now! Now! Now!'"

Change is typically slow. There is great inertia built into any corporate structure. There is an equally strong inertia that keeps each of us locked into our own familiar patterns of thinking and acting. Yet the essence of all change is the recognition of Now! Now! Now! This present moment is the only moment to make the path real.

As authors, we understand this inertia personally. Long before this book got started we talked about Corporate Soul. At that time, few were speaking in the corporate setting about soul, spirit, or meaning as being essential to the "real" business of organizations. We discussed our ideas at length. Although we felt a calling to move forward, months and then a year or two passed with little progress. We delayed our entry to the path, waiting for just the right moment, just the perfect client.

In the end it was not the external conditions that called forth our soulful action. It is simply the recognition of Now! Now! Now! This is the only moment in which to begin the work that is meaningful. For us this meant taking the actions that produced this book and the work in which we are now engaged.

Years ago we read a book on the spiritual life that offered a simple but profound truth: The most important thing is to get on the path, the rest of the steps will come to you once you are on the way.

When You Stumble, Just Keep Going

On a cross-country flight we watched a two-year-old boy turn his mother into a heap of frayed nerves. She was trying to keep him in his seat until the "fasten seat belt sign" was turned off. When the moment of freedom finally came, the boy, liberated from his seat, began to run happily up and down the aisle. As he passed our row the plane hit an "air bump" and jostled slightly. The boy lost his footing and fell over, flat on his face. Both of us stopped breathing. We glanced around quickly and saw several other passengers staring at the small prone figure. As we later discussed, during those brief seconds, both of us imagined how embarrassing it would be to fall flat on our face in front of all those people. But the two-year-old held no such thoughts. He pushed himself up and immediately began to run forward again.

There is little doubt most of us will each stumble as we begin our soul's path. Will that prospect keep us in our seats? Will the spectre of embarrassment be stronger than our desire to be free? Getting started is the key.

Waiting for Certainty

One of India's modern saints, Swami Nityananda, said, "If you are afraid of water, you cannot cross the river even by boat."

If we are afraid of getting started, no tool or technique will seem adequate. Collecting techniques can go on forever. And clearly, there are many tools, techniques, and methods for getting started on the journey to Corporate Soul. This book is not the definitive book on soul at work. There is no such definitive work. Yet our desire for a certain path with clear signals and markers can keep us searching for more information instead of acting on what we already know.

Do not fool yourself and do not try to fool others into thinking that gathering more information will allay all underlying doubts. Action is the ultimate antidote. The most important thing we can do to awaken the Corporate Soul is not to establish a complicated strategy but to begin. In the words of Native American wisdom:

"As you go the way of life, you will see a great chasm. Jump! It is not as wide as you think."

Or as Paige, our skydiving friend, says, "The first step is intense. But after that the view is amazing."

A Framework for Getting Started

In the spirit of a book that has asked as many questions as it has presented answers, we offer a framework for getting started. These are not ten simple steps that everyone or every company must take. Soul is more subtle than this. Rather we suggest three ways to move forward:

1. Sit in silence
2. See the seeds
3. Speak the truth

Sit in Silence

The first step of the journey may not be a step at all but rather a rest stop. The soul starts to awaken when we sit in stillness. The early Christian desert fathers said, "Sit in your cell for the cell will teach you everything." They knew that all the answers lie within the soul. But it is only in stopping and sitting that we can see or hear them.

In stillness we can disengage from the pressures of the to-do list and reflect on the guidance that comes from within. A form of reflective sitting is to return to the 150-percent question we posed back in Chapter 1: Think of a job, project or assignment that brought out 150 percent of your energy and commitment. What made the difference?

If the soul has become dormant at work, reflecting on times when soul was present can make one aware of how to take action so that soul will re-emerge. A CEO we work with has long been known as a visionary leader with the capability of inspiring the best in others. Recently, he took a new assignment at a much larger and more complex organization rife with conflict and complexity. He confided to us that even in the face of this new challenge he was aware the soul had gone out of his work and the job had become only a job.

This is painful for any leader to acknowledge. And when it happens to the CEO the effects of the soul crisis can reverberate in silent ripples throughout the organization. We worked with him to reflect on the 150-percent question and suggested that he live with this question for awhile to identify times when the fire of inspiration and creativity had burned within.

His process reflection revealed several factors missing in his new job that were key to his soul's vitality. One of these was the way in which his new position isolated him from those places in the organization where he felt the real work was being done. By structuring regular opportunities to get out "where the real work is done," he not only rekindled his sense of personal mission, but discovered ways of building community across the organization.

Reflecting Together

Departments and whole organizations can enter into times of reflection together. Such reflection may begin as a series of conversations about soul at work. Many of the exercises in the first few chapters can be used by groups. When people begin to define for themselves what it means to awaken Corporate Soul and honestly discuss how their present workplace compares with this ideal, important work is being done.

Sitting or reflecting can be disconcerting if being busy is the very definition of what it means to be needed or if frenetic activity is the badge of corporate identification. Only in the silence of sitting are we able to gain a perspective that transcends the high speed race of day-to-day work.

Sitting means just what it sounds like. Stop and sit down. Practice mindful breathing. Put yourself into the neutral zone. This is the place of creation, a place of nonmovement from which a new direction can emerge.

A consultant with twenty-five years of experience speaking of the need for more stillness asked, "That is at the heart of it all isn't it? The very nature of the corporation, its incessant busyness and activity, shields it from the engine of soul, which is silence."

At meetings this can mean asking a question and then consciously taking a few minutes to reflect in silence rather than leaping into immediate discussion. It is granting space for such questions on "company" time knowing that the ultimate payoff is a renewed culture able to sustain peak performance.

See the Seeds

Another first step is to begin to see how your current work already awakens your soul and the way the organization supports Corporate Soul. The widespread acceptance of a "Dilbertized" view of the world provides a humorous defense against all that disturbs and aggravates us at work, but the underlying cynicism also shields us from recognizing the seeds of the soul that are growing around us.

Earlier we shared the story of a woman who used a journal to record the blessings she experienced at work, ways in which she felt she had been of service and value.

By paying attention to the seeds of blessing that were already present, she created a new future for herself.

Where are the seeds of soul in your organization? What are the signs of awakening? It is important to see these seeds not as insignificant but as the future "orchards" that they are. The seeds of the soul contain everything. And seeds need to be seen so they can be watered and cared for.

Speak the Truth

Words are powerful. Every tradition points to the generative capacity of speech. In the Old Testament, Adam demonstrates his stewardship of nature by "naming" the beasts and birds. To name something is to give it life from the perspective of the soul. That which is unnamed cannot become part of our life. In Sanskrit the term *vak* (from which we derive the words vocal, vocation, etc.) indicates the creative power of the word. In the yoga tradition there is a recognition that for anything to happen in the world it first must be spoken.

That is why one of the most significant first steps in awakening Corporate Soul has to do with speaking truth both to ourselves and to our companions at work. If we want to awaken Corporate Soul, first we must say so.

This simple act of speaking to ourselves is not as easy or straightforward as it first sounds. When we begin to speak truth about the work we are in, we may discover other voices within us responding. The voices of our latent fears of bankruptcy or unemployment may make themselves heard. Other parts of us that have become accustomed to, if not satisfied by the corporate life, may even tell us to deny the emerging truth that we must make a change.

Find people, soul allies, to whom you can speak. Begin a deeper conversation. This speaking will cause ideas to flow and momentum to build. Jesus sent his disciples out in pairs for a reason—because the task is not easy alone.

A Sufi story tells of a blind man who had spent the evening at a friend's house. After dinner and conversation were concluded the blind man prepared to leave. "Here," said the host. "Let me give you this lighted candle for your walk home."

"Good friend," said the blind man. "This light will do me no good, for my eyes are veiled in darkness."

"Yes," said the host, "but the light may serve to alert others of your approach."

The blind man left with the candle. He felt his way steadily along the familiar streets of the village. After some time the blind man collided with another man who was running in his direction.

"What are you doing?!" yelled the blind man. "Can't you see the candle I am carrying?"

"Sir," replied the other, "your light has gone out."

When we speak our truth in the organization we serve both purposes highlighted in this Sufi tale. First, we hold out a light to which others can respond. People in your organization may be waiting for someone to say what must be said and begin the process of change. Speaking the truth can be the light that calls others to join you in a quest for greater engagement.

Yet our speaking also invites the voices of others to give us feedback. By beginning an honest dialogue we open up to others. They then can tell us when they see that our light has gone out and also when they see it burning brightly.

If we keep our vision of a more soulful work place at the level of thought, we have, in a sense, trapped the soul's energy in a cage of abstraction. We need to speak our truth. To speak is to put breath behind our thoughts. It is to breathe life into them. As we speak our private visions become collective property and we set the stage for more tangible manifestation.

Dragons on the Path

All the wisdom traditions tell us that there are obstacles and challenges along the path. These are symbolized in the form of dragons, demons, and monsters. The path to awakening the Corporate Soul is no different. As we endeavor to create more soulful corporate cultures, we will encounter dragons.

The traditions also tell us that even when the dragons appear to be outside us that is only an optical illusion. The real dragons are inside. These are the dragons that pull us from the path of our deepest intentions and cause us to lose contact with the soul.

The Dragon of Security

One of the most powerful dragons on the path to Corporate Soul is our desire for security. This can manifest itself as a desire to be taken care of, or as a clinging to financial or job security. This dragon makes us afraid to take risks and pursue our deeper values; it parades fearsome images before our inner mind. We see ourselves losing our place on the corporate ladder. We envision our bank account draining away. Everything appears unstable and uncertain so we grasp more tightly to what we have. Leaders may fear that while they spend time nurturing Corporate Soul, their competitors will focus on more rational efforts and take over the market.

As authors, we had our own bouts with this dragon. We knew clients were interested in reengineering and in customer service, but weren't certain they would be interested in nurturing Corporate Soul. If we associated ourselves with something so seemingly "soft," would we be banished to the new-age never-never land along with a reduction in fees as a penalty for proffering silly fluff? These fears kept driving us back to the security of work we knew we could sell even when we wanted to offer something deeper.

Like all dragons, the dragon of security can become an ally or an enemy. Dragons on the path are basically just powerful energies. They are tremendous sources of power that when tamed can serve us well, but when unchecked will take over and destroy our lives. Tamed, the dragon of security can speak with the voice of practicality. This friendly dragon asks us to ground our vision of what might be with a recognition of our own and others limitations. This tamed dragon helps us move forward on the path without damaging ourselves in the process. This dragon reminds us that the mortgage must be paid and keeps our feet on the ground as we move toward a more soulful workplace. But when the dragon of security is untamed, it takes over and consumes our sense of adventure. We dry up and we stop growing.

Recognizing the terrifying visions of personal and professional disaster that arise in our minds as the untamed ravings of the security dragon can give us some much-needed perspective. This dragon's goal is to keep us safe no matter what—even if that means never changing or growing. Taming our dragons is different from slaying them. It is fundamentally unwise to kill any of the dragons. They are part of us and to kill them is to kill part of ourselves. But we do want to tame them so that their powerful energy can be used to further the journey of awakening.

The Dragon of Impatience

As we move along the paths to Corporate Soul we may meet the dragon of impatience. This dragon comes in the form of our desire for quick results. Of course this restless energy gets in the way of fruitful spiritual work. We get fed up and blame others, then either give up or move on. This dragon pushes us to change jobs and seek greener pastures, instead of staying where we are and doing the hard work that is required to develop and nurture self, community, craft, and contribution.

The dragon of impatience can make us abort our soul path when it does not magically transform all problems overnight. When we are in the grip of this dragon we are like a person who is digging for water. We dig down four feet and go to another location when we find no water. There we dig another shallow hole and are again frustrated to find nothing. But water is never found by digging fifty shallow wells. Only by staying with the process and one-pointed action is the water of the soul found.

The dragon of impatience is valuable in that it reminds us of what we really want. This dragon is thirsty for the water of the soul. It is ready for change. But when that readiness is untamed it becomes restlessness. Then we end up moving around a lot but essentially going nowhere.

We tame this dragon of impatience by growing roots and by committing ourselves to blooming where we are planted. We tame this dragon by extending our timeline beyond the immediate.

According to a Chinese proverb, "The tree that is planted often does not grow roots." Soul does not awaken and blossom in haste nor does an organization transform itself according to our neat and orderly timelines (in spite of our many Gantt charts outlining the phases of change).

When we began our own path to Corporate Soul, a funny thing began to happen: The phones stopped ringing, not a good thing in the consulting and corporate speaking business. It is a sign that your name and your place in the market are weakening. To stay on the path during these times of darkness and apparent inactivity requires a clear and compelling vision that becomes the psychological light at the end of the tunnel that draws us forward. During these periods of silence it was tempting to give up and turn back. The journey of awakening rarely provides instant gratification. It is an organic process; we can push the river all we want, but the river will move at its own rhythm.

Certainly this is also true of organizational transformation. A series of seminars on corporate soul will not instantaneously awaken the slumbering giant. Our efforts will bring results but will often require tremendous patience. One of the leaders we work with tried for two years to change the culture of the organization he inherited with little apparent result. He was almost ready to abandon his efforts when he attended a meeting . It was obvious through listening to the people at that meeting the years of effort were finally paying off. A new organization was emerging just before he was ready to move on.

The Dragon of Popularity

The untamed dragon of popularity is another impediment to awakening the Corporate Soul. Transforming our workplace requires challenging some sacred cows. Unwelcome truths will have to be spoken to ourselves and to others. We may find ourselves ignored, blamed, and laughed at, as well as applauded, rewarded, and enshrined! We must be prepared for both.

But the dragon of popularity desires a one-sided reception. This dragon craves acknowledgment and appreciation. And through this craving the truthfulness needed to build a community that nurtures Corporate Soul can be undermined. This dragon will blunt our words, soft-pedal our ideas, and spin-doctor our insights so they seem safe and palatable. The dragon of popularity can turn the most powerful truth into a vapid slogan. This dragon talks in buzz words and keeps us from removing our corporate mask to speak about our deeper desires for the organization.

But like the other dragons this one too has a useful energy to offer us. The dragon of popularity provides us with sensitivity to other points of view. When tamed, this dragon helps us understand how others think and guides us in phrasing our ideas so that they will be most easily understood. The dragon of popularity when tamed provides us with empathy for others' viewpoints and feelings without causing us to distort our message to make it acceptable.

The Dragon of Doubt

Perhaps the most powerful dragon on the path is doubt. Shakespeare said, "Our doubts are like traitors, betraying the good we might otherwise do!" The New Testament says, "All things are possible if one only believes."

Yet how many of us honestly believe that our company could be a place that calls forth the deepest energies within us? How many of us believe that our work will be an expression of the soul?

The dragon of doubt keeps us stuck in a compromised vision. This dragon tells us, "Be realistic; smell the coffee, and wake up from your childish dream." This dragon confronts us with images of the people in our organization. It says, "Do you really think these people care about soul?" When we are in the grip of this dragon, everyone looks greedy, self-serving, and completely absorbed in their own agendas. The result is that we give up on awakening Corporate Soul and live for the weekends.

But even the dragon of doubt can be tamed. And when it is, this dragon becomes a powerful ally. When doubt is tamed it becomes discrimination. This dragon, now tamed, has the ability to see through the corporate masks to the soul that lies buried in others. This tamed dragon of discrimination focuses us on those actions that will produce real change and discards those that are merely cosmetic. This dragon of discrimination helps us to sharpen our vision into something we not only believe in but upon which we cannot resist acting.

The Journey Begins

Taming dragons is ongoing work. Awakening the soul takes more than a three-day workshop. It is ever-present work. Heraclitus said, "You could never arrive at the limits of the soul, no matter how many roads you traveled, so deep is its mystery."

To step upon the path of awakening is to accept the soul's mystery. It is to merge into a creative process that includes and transcends our personal life. When this happens something magical happens. Even in the midst of daily challenges and demands we can echo Meister Eckhart's words: "We are fellow-helpers with God, co-creators in everything we do."

It is possible to wait for the perfect job, the perfect opportunity, the perfect first step to move toward soul at work. This was certainly true for us. It was almost three years ago now that we began wondering if there could be more in our work with our clients—a deeper calling that revolved around the discovery of soul at work. For some time we did nothing but talk about getting on the path, strategizing and reading in preparation for the first steps. Now, three years later, we wish we had just started writing the first week, started talking to our clients, integrating the soul into our present work. For as we have taken steps, other steps, mentors, and paths have unfolded that were never seen at the trail's edge.

We wondered how to end this book but realized a book about soul can never have a final word. Like a finger pointing at the moon, these pages can only indicate where to look to find Corporate Soul. The end of this story will not be written by us. It will be realized in your life and your work. The pen is now in your hands.

Eight Ways to Start Awakening Corporate Soul

1. Answer the 150-percent question for yourself. Identify two ways you can create more of what brings your energy out in your work.
2. Find a way to get closer to customers. Go out and talk to them, videotape them, phone them—remind yourself and others of the difference you make.
3. Provide a development program that gets staff looking at what their skills and passions are—help them take responsibility for creating these things at work.
4. Plan ways for people to get to know each other beyond their function (for example, the name tag exercise in this handout). Do it at a staff meeting.
5. Reframe your work as an organization/unit to a "sound bite" that is about something noble. Use these words consistently.
6. Identify a new skill/area of expertise you'd like to explore. Find a project that brings you into a new arena. Constantly look for ways to give staff the opportunity to do the same. (One simple way is to have people trade jobs!)
7. Begin a list of things you are grateful for in your work day—ways you feel you have contributed—then look at the pattern and work at creating more of those kinds of things.
8. Identify a truth that should be said in your organization. Find allies and begin to speak the truth.

Exercise: What Is Your Legacy?

Take a few minutes and pretend that your work career ended right now (or if you prefer, that the company, division, and so forth, that you lead went out of business right now). As you reflect back on your career and/or your organizations history, what do you regret in terms of "soul." What was not done? What was less than you would like? If it could be done again, what would you have liked to be true?

_____

_____

_____

_____

_____

_____

_____

_____

_____

_____

_____

_____

If you are so inclined, write an epithet of missed opportunity and wishes about work/workplace.

_____

_____

_____

_____

_____

_____

_____

_____

_____

_____

_____

Exercise: Making Friends of Dragons

There are many dragons at the entrance to the paths to corporate soul. We identified a few of them: security, impatience, popularity, and doubt. What fears do you have regarding walking the paths to Corporate Soul for yourself and your company?

_____
_____
_____
_____
_____
_____
_____
_____
_____
_____

What can you do to transform your fears and get started?

_____
_____
_____
_____
_____
_____
_____
_____
_____
_____

Exercise: How You Will Begin

The final exercise of this book is the first chapter in your own journey toward awakening the Corporate Soul. Remember there are no perfect steps. Identify what you will do in the next week to begin the journey. If you see yourself as a leader within your organization, find steps that can move your company toward deeper commitment. If your focus is more personal, then find ways to renew your personal sense of vocation.

Steps I will take for myself.

_____

_____

_____

_____

_____

_____

_____

_____

_____

_____

_____

Steps I will take in and for my organization.

_____

_____

_____

_____

_____

_____

_____

_____

_____

_____

_____

We have always found action occurs most often and consistently when we are accountable to others. Find a trusted colleague and share your commitments. Arrange a time to meet in thirty to forty-five days to reflect on your progress.

My plans for achieving Corporate Soul
over the next week:

_____

_____

_____

_____

_____

_____

_____

_____

_____

_____

_____

_____

_____

_____

_____

_____

_____

_____

_____

_____

_____

My plans for achieving Corporate Soul
over the next year:

_____

_____

_____

_____

_____

_____

_____

_____

_____

_____

_____

_____

_____

_____

_____

_____

_____

_____

_____

_____

_____

_____

_____

Corporate Soul
Services & Networks

Your personal and organizational journey to Corporate Soul can be accelerated by connecting with others on the path.The authors offer the following methods for you to become part of the growing network of people commited to awakening Corporate Soul:

Leadership Retreats

Retreats are for those who want to devote uninterrupted time to personal renewal and Corporate Soul awakening.

Newsletter

To add your name to our Newletter list e-mail us at info@izzoconsulting.com

Speaking and Consulting

John Izzo speaks at more than 100 events globally each year. To request information on consulting, training or to make an inquiry into speaking availability please call us **at: 604-913-0649** or e-mail us at **info@izzoconsulting.com**.

To reach Dr. John Izzo
Corporate Office:

Izzo Consulting, Inc.
200 Isleview Place
PO Box 668
Lions Bay, BC Canada V0N 2E0
604-913-0649
fax: 604-913-0648
website: www.izzoconsulting.com
e-mail: info@izzoconsulting.com

To reach Eric Klein
1455 Hymettus Avenue
Encinitas, CA 92024 USA
760/436-5535
Fax 760/634-3589
eklein@dharmaconsulting.com

Other Books by Dr. John Izzo

Values Shift: The New Work Ethic and What it Means for Business
By John Izzo and Pam Withers

One workplace, three generations and six values they all have in common. Retaining the most talented people requires aligning their values with those of the organization. This critically acclaimed book will give you insightful information on what other companies are doing to respond to these shifts and the culture changes it has produced.

Decrease your retention, get more from your people and build a culture based on real-time values.

Suggested Reading

Stewardship by Peter Block

Toa of Leadership by John Heider

Wherever You Go There You Are: Mindfulness Meditation in Everyday Life by Jon Kabat-Zinn

The Power of Purpose: Creating Meaning in Your Life and Work by Richard Leider

Mastery by George Leonard

Care of the Soul: A Guide to Cultivating Depth and Sacredness in Everyday Life by Thomas Moore

Time and the Soul by Jacob Needleman

Loving Kindness by Sharon Saulzbury Zen at Work by Les Kaye

Management of the Absurd by Richard Fardson

Don't Sweat the Small Stuff by Richard Carlson

Corporate Soul

Learning the Practices and Tools for Personal and Organizational Renewal

Do These Statements Describe You?

• You know that the challenges of leadership require deep change not a quick fix.
• You are passionate about bringing more spirit to the workplace.
• You want to bring spirituality more fully into the work you do.
• You seek an approach to enrich your work and workplace that is practical.

Based on the book Awakening Corporate Soul: Four Paths to Unleash the Power of People at Work, this workshop provides a solid set of practices and principles. The practices taught are based on 2000 interviews with people from all walks of life, about what creates high performance and high fulfillment at work.

Benefits of Attending

For individuals:
•Gain increased vitality and clarity of purpose in your work.
•Discover your own high performance/high fulfillment equation.
•Learn the practices for bringing your purpose alive on a daily basis.
•Renew and sharpen your leadership vision.

For organizations:
•Explore the Four Paths to Corporate Soul: This model brings the power of the wisdom traditions to organizational change.
•Learn team practices for creating full engagement: Practical methods for applying soul solutions to organizational problems.

Learning at a Deeper Level

This workshop is designed to go from the inside-out. Participants will experience personal renewal in their work while learning models for creating renewal within organizations and teams. The core practices of renewal include:

- Mindfulness: the secret to flow
- Taming the dragons that drain the soul at work
- 150 percent engagement: the performance fulfillment model
- Building communities of purpose
- Enhancing the power of contribution and service
- Understanding core values and legacy
- The Renewal Cycle: how to let go and create
- The power of stories and truth telling
- Bringing more artistry into daily work

Who Should Attend

- Leaders who want to create an environment that brings out the best in people
- Consultants/trainers (internal and external) who want to help leaders and organizations transform
- Professionals who want to renew their sense of purpose and bring more soul to their work

To register or for more information please call 1-604-913-0649. Visa, Mastercard, and corporate checks accepted.